Published by Writer's Publishing House
publishing@gwm.services
https://writerspublishinghouse.com

Cover Created by Writer's Publishing House

Edited by Ghost Writer Media Staff

Shadows of the Past – Carmichael Lewis

ISBN 978-1-7335551-3-5

Carmichael Lewis Copyright © 2020 All Rights Reserved

All rights reserved. No part of this book may be reproduced in whole or in part, without the written permission of the publisher except by a reviewer who may quote brief passages in a review; nor may any part of this book be reproduced or transmitted in any form or by any means, electronic or mechanical, including photocopying recording, or by any information storage and retrieval system, without the written permission of the publisher.

Shadows of the Past
The Path to Greatness

By Carmichael Lewis

Table of Contents

Introduction 5

Author Bio 6

Chapter One: 8
    A New Beginning 8

Chapter Two: 24
    Uncertain Outcomes 24

Chapter Three: 30
    Minimal Options 30

Chapter Four: 49
    Waiting 49

Chapter Five: 61
    Ocean Breeze 61

Chapter Six: 81
    The Final Results 81

Chapter Seven: 84
    New Life 84

Chapter Eight: 98

Things Happen for a Reason 98

Chapter Nine: 111

    Expecting 111

Chapter Ten: 122

    The Recurring Event 122

Chapter Eleven: 125

    In the Moment 125

Chapter Twelve: 133

    It's Almost Time 133

Chapters Thirteen: 144

    In the Blink of an Eye 144

Chapters Fourteen: 151

    Little Angel 151

Chapter Fifteen: 162

    Going Home 162

Introduction

It is my sincere hope this book will help influence positive change in one's personal and professional life. This book is about the love you give and how it is returned abundantly. If you are looking for a change, or the motivation to overcome any obstacle, please keep reading. My story is about a young boy who had no guidance and no one to guide him along the way, besides the bad decisions of a lonely youth looking for a way to fit in.

The key is to stay focused on your goals, dreams and aspirations and nothing can stop you. The story tells how a boy became a man through adversity and lessons learned.

Carmichael wore a mask to hide the scars of his past, but through all the hardships he became a highly decorated man; his passion for helping others came from the lack of help he experienced as a youth. In turn, he believes the greatest value is helping others reach their potential, so that they will pass on the same passion to others to contribute to making this world a better place.

Author Bio

Carmichael is the founder of a fitness brand in Chicago, and he recognizes the value of education. Therefore, with his master's degree in Public Safety Administration and bachelor's degree in Criminal Justice, he supplements his professional experience with innovative educational opportunities to broaden his knowledge base.

Carmichael realized at a young age that health was important, especially being in law enforcement. He became a certified personal trainer, so that he could help people look and feel their best. His personal training extends to upcoming candidates who are inspired to become officers. He takes them through a fitness test and mentors them through the hiring process. The personal satisfaction he gets from his fitness training led him to create his fitness brand, and with that he promotes a healthier lifestyle with the community and youths in Chicago.

Carmichael is currently a law enforcement officer in Chicago. He began his career in 2008, and he spent his first five years of service in the suburbs of Chicago. He has received many awards including honorable mentions, life-saving, distinguished officer and one of the highest awards from the department, the Award of Valor. Carmichael's passion for youth and the community is so strong that he volunteers at local schools, speaking to young people about violence, gangs and becoming a person of value.

As the only one of his siblings to achieve a higher education, he recognizes the importance of education to improve your life. The health and wellness of others is an important part of Carmichael's peace of mind. Yet, he still wanted more, so he decided to write his first book, which is based on a true story. He looks forward to a promising writing career and emphasizes his dedication to the community he currently serves.

Chapter One:

A New Beginning

"You may kiss the bride," the pastor stated.

Julian lifted his bride's veil, and her beauty caught him off guard. The image was pure perfection; nothing could have prepared him for this moment. She captivated his heart from the moment he laid eyes on her in that café. By the time they had their first date, he knew she would be the perfect mate. People always mock love at first sight, but to Julian they were wrong. He spent much of his adulthood running from the past, fighting to free himself from the incidents that had plagued his life.

Aniyah changed everything. Her very presence lit up his existence. "I love you," Julian whispered.

His bride smiled, "I love you too!" The delicate kiss exhilarated Julian; he could taste the strawberry essence of her lipstick.

Their guests clapped as the married couple turned to face the world for the first time as one unit. Julian firmly grasped her hand as they walked down the aisle of the church. He felt like the heavens had blessed him unbelievably. All the heartache and trepidation of the past vanished. It was an overwhelming emotional rollercoaster.

As the couple walked outside, Julian felt the warmth radiating across his face. The day brought a whole new beginning. Tucked close to his side was Aniyah, his wife. A life filled with promise awaited.

Their first destination was Hawaii for a two-week honeymoon. Julian made arrangements with his staff to watch over business affairs while they were away. Gym Addict Apparel ranked just under 10 in national sales last month. Julian had married the love of his life. The chapter was closed, and his new life was beginning.

It was an exhilarating time for both parties. Neither one had traveled much in their lifetimes, so experiencing this trip together made it more worthwhile. They were eager to get the travel over with and relax on the beach in Hawaii. The destination was Ka'anapali Beach Hotel, Hawaii's most authentic hotel resort.

Julian had arranged a limo to and from the airport. In the limo waited strawberries and champagne with chocolate truffles if so desired. Julian figured you only get married once and it should be the most special day of your life. Plus, if you happen to marry the love of your life, that just makes it better.

"Honey… you shouldn't have! It is incredible! Are you sure we can afford to have all this stuff?" Aniyah asked.

"Yes, I have saved for the last year to take you on a trip like this, we will be fine. Don't worry. It's our honeymoon, let's enjoy ourselves," Julian told her.

"Okay. If you are sure, I won't worry, then."

"Great! Shall we, my lady?" Julian knew the trip cost a great deal, but business was good and he could afford something this special for his bride.

Aniyah sat next to the window, sipping her champagne. She didn't drink much, so it was a treat to have something special. She had to admit the strawberries and champagne were amazing.

The limo ride was thrilling for both newlyweds. It was the first time either one had experienced such luxury. Plus, having a chauffeur driving through the streets of Chicago was wonderful.

As the limo stopped next to the curb at O'Hare Airport and the newlyweds exited the car, Aniyah realized the effects of the champagne.

"Whoo, Julian, I'm feeling a buzz from my drink in the limo."

Julian laughed, "Well, maybe you can take a nap, since we have a six-hour flight?" She nodded in agreement.

The couple made their way through the airport. After a quick thirty-minute wait in the terminal, they boarded the plane.

The plane prepared for takeoff, while the flight attendants walked the aisle assisting passengers.

"Miss, can I get a pillow for my wife?" Julian asked the attendant.

"Absolutely, just a moment." The flight attendant went to get a pillow and returned quickly.

"Here you are, can I get you anything else?"

"No, I believe we are good. Thank you." She nodded.

"Are you sure it won't bother you if I sleep for a while?"

"Not at all honey, get some rest. You are going to need it once we land. I will just read my book."

Julian grabbed his book, but found himself lost in thought over the wedding and the most beautiful woman sleeping next to him. He could not help thinking how God had provided him with the perfect mate; not in a million years could he have chosen someone so special.

The hours flew by as Julian reminisced over his past. But, the nagging in his gut demanded he listen. At some point he would have to tell his bride about the mistakes he'd made and hope she understood. He had wanted to explain many times, but finding the courage was impossible.

The pilot announced they would be landing in Hawaii within the next fifteen minutes. "Aniyah, we are going to land, honey. Wake up." She peeked one eye open and smiled.

"Are we here already?" Julian nodded.

The newlyweds landed exhausted, but ready to feel the warm ocean breeze. It was an experience they could not feel in Chicago.

They remained quiet on the drive to the resort, lost in personal thought over the experience. They had been a couple for several years, so spending time together was not unusual. Aniyah knew Julian very well and respected his dedication to life and their relationship. He worked diligently on his career, achieving one accomplishment after another. But, his most prized triumph was giving back to the community. Part of the proceeds of his athletic clothing company were used to empower youth and encourage a healthier lifestyle, something Julian was very passionate about.

The limo arrived at the resort, and waiting in front was the bellhop ready to escort them to their suite: a
private lanai (balcony) room overlooking the Maui beachfront.

"Right this way, sir," the bellhop stated.

"Thank you," Julian replied. The warm breeze blowing off the ocean was tantalizing, caressing their skin with a delicate allure.

Aniyah paused outside the hotel to smell the ocean air filtering through the lush green environment. "Are you coming?" Julian asked.

"No, go ahead. I'll be right here." She wanted nothing more than to grab her bikini and head to the beach.

"Alright, I'll be back soon." Julian sent a staff member to set up a chair and drink for his wife to enjoy and then headed to the front desk to take care of business. Aniyah waited outside the hotel on the front lawn for an employee to bring her a chair and drink. She was grateful to be in such a beautiful place with the man she loved.

"Thank you for bringing a chair; can I have a drink with an umbrella? No alcohol, please," she asked the waiter.

"Yes, ma'am. Right away."

Aniyah loved the individual pampering. It wasn't often she got to enjoy the luxury of someone waiting on her for a change. She grew up in a large family and was the oldest of six siblings. Both of her parents worked long hours to support the family, and they depended on her to take care of her siblings. Raised in the suburbs of a lower-class area, it was a difficult adolescence. But she was always loved by her parents; they wanted the best for all their children. It was hard on Aniyah when she lost her aunt several years ago. Then, last year, her father took ill, and they almost lost him as well. She was the first in her family to graduate from college with a degree. Aniyah loved children and always wanted to help; it was her way of giving back. The previous year she had graduated and began work as a social worker. It was a perfect match with Julian's passion for the community.

"Honey…" Julian called.

"Ahhhh," she jumped. Lost in thought over the last few days, he startled her.

"I'm sorry, I didn't mean to scare you."

"It's alright. Are we all checked in now?" she asked.

"Yes, would you like to head for the beach? We can order dinner and eat down at the beach."

"Really? Yes, let's go."

"Alright, we'll go change and pre-order dinner for later." The two eagerly hopped upstairs and prepped for their meal beachside.

Aniyah had bought a new bikini for the trip to surprise Julian, along with other unmentionables that shall remain private. The sight left Julian speechless, which did not happen often. "Wow! You look fantastic," he announced.

"Oh stop. Thank you," she replied, his stare making her blush. "Come on… daylight is waning," she grinned. Julian loved her sense of humor; he could be himself with no judgment.

This was something he had never experienced until Aniyah came into his life. But some secrets are better left in the past.

"Race ya!" Aniyah shouted.

"Really… you think so?" he said proudly.

"Yep!" She darted for the beach. They spent so much time taking care of everyone else it was fun to relax and just have fun.

The deep sand on the beach left them both panting, but Aniyah got the better of Julian today. "I cannot believe I beat you!" she stated.

"Yeah, I know. Next time, you won't stand a chance."

"Are you alright?" She looked concerned.

"I'm good. Just tired. It's been a long few days."

"Perfect reason to lie in the sun and just relax. If we get hot, the water is right there to cool off. Or, we can hit the area covered with umbrellas." Julian smiled; it all sounded fantastic. They spent the afternoon sipping virgin Mai Tais, with the occasional dip in the ocean.

Dinner brought seared sea bass with lemon, olives, and white beans, served with a sunset overlooking the ocean. It was a magical place to end the perfect day.

"If I know you, Julian Parker, you must have something planned for tomorrow."

"Haha, yes you know me too well! A hike on the Stairway to Heaven trail. It's 3,922 stairs and has a 2000-foot elevation, so it should prove interesting," he said.

"Are you sure? It's our honeymoon. Do we want to work that hard?"

"If you're chicken, you can stay here," he stated in jest. Julian knew she never backed down from anything.

"Alright. You only live once, right?"

"Yep," he stated.

"We'll if we're hiking in the morning, we better get some rest."

"Maybe not just sleep," Julian winked. Aniyah blushed.

The front desk promptly rang their room at 6:00 a.m. The limo arrived at 7:30 a.m. Julian rented their hiking equipment from the hotel since their own gear was at home. They both knew the importance of being prepared when participating in any physical activities.

"Good morning, may I help you with your things?" The driver asked.

"Yes, please," they replied.

"You are heading to Heaven Oahu today? Should be a beautiful day for that hike," he told them.

"Great! We are looking forward to the views," Julian answered.

"Yes, they are beautiful. Just be very careful. Parts of the stairway are dangerous. I have hiked it many times myself."

"Thank you, we will. We are experienced hikers." The driver nodded. However, Julian agreed that the hike looked intimidating from the pictures he saw online.

Their drive to the Oahu hiking trail was impressive. Some sights along Lolii Drive were unbelievable. The two newlyweds ate breakfast during the drive, a quick high protein meal for energy on the trail.

Julian watched his bride enjoy her scrambled eggs and slice of turkey. It amazed him to be in the presence of such a wonderful woman. No matter how many days he saw the sunrise, her company would never get boring.

"Just call me when you're about halfway down, and I'll come to pick you up, okay?" the driver asked.

"Yes, thank you. See you this afternoon," Aniyah replied.

They prepped their packs and grabbed the hiking poles. "Ready?" Julian questioned.

"Yep, let's go."

The breath-taking view slowed their progress up the staircase. But who could pass up the photo ops? "Come on. Julian, we need a selfie of both of us with the island in the background."

Julian agreed and made his way back to Aniyah's side. She held the camera up and snapped the photo. "Hold up just a second. I want to post this right away." Julian nodded.

"Okay, I'm ready. Julian…." she called out. Silence.

Aniyah turned to look when Julian failed to respond. She had her back to him, as the glare from the sun interfered with her view of the screen.

"Julian!" she screamed. Aniyah rushed to his side as he collapsed.

Julian fell over the rail onto a grassy section along the path. He was conscious and breathing, but unresponsive. Aniyah patted his cheek. "Julian… can you hear me?" she repeated in succession. Her attempts to revive him failed. She gently took off her pack and rested it under his head so she could call 911.

"911 can I help you?" the operator asked.

"Yes, I am on Heaven Oahu trail, and my husband collapsed. He is breathing but not conscious. He won't respond."

"Alright, I need you to stay on the line while I dispatch help. Does your husband have any medical issues?"

"I don't think so, he never said anything. We were just married and on our honeymoon."

"Alright, does your husband have any issues with heart problems in his family?"

"I am not sure, but I don't know that much about his family. Julian is adamant about his health, so I can't imagine he would."

"Oh… I am sorry. Please stay with me, help is on the way. Is your husband still breathing?

"No… I don't think so…"

"Check for a pulse. Do you know how?" the operator asked.

"Yes, just a minute." Aniyah checked his wrist for a pulse. "It's faint, but he has one," she stated.

"Great! You're doing wonderfully. Help is about ten minutes away. There is a heliport pad just up from your location. They will land there and hike down to where you are. Stay on the line with me until help arrives. Plus, with the signal we can track your location."

"Alright, I will hold with you."

"What is your name?" the operator asked.

"Umm… Aniyah."

"Wow, that is a beautiful name. Where are you from?"

"I live in Chicago. We wanted to see Hawaii, so it was perfect for our honeymoon. Is help coming…?" She started to sob.

"Yes, you should hear the helicopter soon."

Aniyah waited patiently for help to arrive, and she watched the future fade from sight. The love of her life lay static in her arms, on the top of a mountain. "Julian… Please come back to me..." she prayed.

Moments later she heard the helicopter coming over the horizon. She breathed a sigh of relief.

"Julian, do you see? Help is on the way. Please stay with me!" she pleaded.

The first responders waved to acknowledge they found them on the hillside. It would still be some time before they would reach their position, but at least assistance was coming.

Chapter Two:

Uncertain Outcomes

Aniyah sat in the hospital room watching a machine breathe for her husband. Their new life hung in the balance. Only time would tell the tale of Julian's prognosis. She found herself in a strange land, unfamiliar territory. It was her dream since childhood to travel the world, but after recent events, it may become a pastime she'd choose to avoid. The last thing she wanted was to associate travel with the time when the love of her life died.

"Hi, are you Mrs. Parker?" the doctor asked.

"Yes, I am. Is he alright? What happened?" she asked fearfully.

"I am afraid Julian has coronary artery disease. It is a weakening of the heart. It's something he has had from birth, but in many cases, it does not affect the person until adulthood. He probably was not aware of the symptoms. If he grew up with this problem, the indications would be a normal part of life."

"How serious is the problem?" she asked.

"We are running some more tests to find out the extent of the damage. We have him heavily sedated, but he should be awake tomorrow. I'll update you soon. Try to get some rest, ok?"

"Thank you, I will. Can I stay here with Julian?"

"Absolutely. I will send someone to get you settled."

Aniyah's worst fears were coming true. She fell into the chair. Her mind blank, the only thing she could do was cry. "The doctor says you want to stay in the room, right?" a nurse came in and asked.

She nodded, her sobs keeping her from responding verbally.

The nurse returned sometime later with a portable cot for Aniyah to sleep on. It was uncomfortable, but Aniyah did not want to be anywhere else. She tried to ignore the rumblings in her stomach. The last meal she'd eaten was before the hike. Since then, she'd been in the ER.

Aniyah knew she had to call home and inform the families, a task she was not eager to complete. How would she tell them of Julian's fate?

The exhaustion of the last twenty-four hours took over, and the next thing Aniyah knew a priest gently nudging her arm to wake her. "Uhhh" she muttered.

"I am sorry. Are you Mrs. Parker?" the priest asked.

"Yes, father." Aniyah jumped to her feet, stumbling to Julian's side, thinking the worst had happened while she slept.

"Easy, it's alright. Your husband is fine. The doctor thought it might be a good idea for us to speak since you are in Hawaii alone."

"Oh… Father, thank you, but I believe we are alright. I am sure we'll be headed home next week."

"Well if you need anything else, please don't hesitate to ask. I have an office in the hospital and weekly office hours of 8 a.m. -5p.m., but you can always speak to a staff member to contact me in an emergency. But I will come by over the weekend and check on you again."

"Thank you very much, that's very sweet."

Aniyah watched the priest leave the room, wearing a pleasant expression. All the while, she was dying inside. The unknown was taking a toll on her mind. A few moments later, the phone rang. "Hello?" she said.

"Aniyah, it's Sofia. How are you?"

"Sis, I miss you. It's awful. I can't believe this happened. One minute he was fine and the next minute I see him flipping over the rail. I mean, when it comes to fitness Julian is adamant."

"I know, sweetie. It will be alright. You know I'm here if you need anything."

"Thanks. Mom is supposed to call me later. I love you…"

"I love you too, call me when the tests come back, ok?"

"Yes, first thing. Thank you. I love you…" Aniyah hated being alone in a strange place. Her family was always close and being apart was hard.

The nurses came in to change the sheets and take care of Julian, so they suggested she get some dinner and stretch her legs. If anything happened, she would be notified immediately. Food actually sounded good; it had been days since she had eaten anything substantial.

She made sure to kiss her husband on the forehead before leaving. The cafeteria felt like another continent away, but her muscles needed to move; the stiffness had settled deep after hiking then being cooped up in a hospital room. It was hard to walk down the hallway and not break down crying when someone passed by. All she wanted was to talk to her husband and tell him one more time, "I love you!"

The experience taught her a valuable lesson: Never take your loved ones for granted, because they may not be around the next minute. It was a horrible thought, but she knew the prognosis was bleak. Aniyah prayed for the best but expected the worst.

As she made her way downstairs to the cafeteria, the change of scenery lifted her spirits. Her mind raced with a multitude of scenarios, none of which she wanted to deal with alone. The cafeteria was empty at this time of day, and for that she was grateful.

"What can I get you?" the attendant asked.

"Just a large chef's salad, with chicken please?"

"Alright, anything to drink? And do you want dressing?"

"Large coffee, and oil and vinegar."

"Just one moment, please."

The attendant brought her a large coffee and then returned after a few minutes with her chef's salad. It looked delicious.

"Thanks."

"That will be $ 10.50 please."

"Oh, yes." Aniyah paid for her meal and found a table by the windows, overlooking the hillside. The sun had almost disappeared below the horizon. She imagined Julian sitting across the table telling her not to worry, everything would be alright. He was the most positive, uplifting person she'd ever met; he always knew what to say. "I can't imagine…" she paused her thoughts.

Chapter Three:

Minimal Options

Aniyah slept between nurses entering to check monitors and Julian's vitals. Needless to say, her fatigue settled deep. She grabbed a protein bar from the vending machine to take care of breakfast. The doctor would be in at about seven to update her on his prognosis. Maybe then she could get a break and head to the hotel for a shower and clean clothes. The bar tasted good with a coffee from the nurse's station.

"Good morning, Mrs. Parker," the doctor stated.

"Please, call me Aniyah," she said.

"Aniyah. That is a beautiful name," he told her.

"Thank you, it's an old family name."

"Well, the test results were about what I expected. The coronary artery disease is worse than I hoped to see, but we do have an option. He is eligible for a transplant, as Julian is in great health, and he does not drink or smoke.

We can get him on the list right away if you decide to take that route. He should be awake this afternoon, and you both can discuss the options."

"Options? What other options are there? Can this be treated somehow?"

"No, I am afraid not. The heart muscle is too weak. Maybe if this had been treated as a young child, but not at this point. I am sorry."

"As a child? He was born with this, doctor?"

"Yes, coronary artery disease is a birth defect. The severity varies between individuals."

"Ummm, I don't know what to say. This is a nightmare. What are his chances with a transplant?"

"Well, that is the good part. He would most likely make a full recovery and live a long life."

"And, without?" she stammered.

The doctor paused. "The damage is fatal. He will not survive without a new heart."

Aniyah felt the air escape her lungs, and she gasped to breathe. "Oh my God!" she exclaimed.

"Aniyah... Aniyah can you hear me?" she heard the utterances of sound, but her vision remained blurry. Nothing made sense.

"Aniyah..." She heard the nurse say.

She nodded her head. "Yes?"

"You scared us for a few moments," the doctor stated.

"What happened?"

"You passed out and almost hit your head on the edge of the bed. Dr. Mc Carthy caught you just in time."

"How long have I been out?"

"About five minutes."

"The last thing I remember is him saying Julian needs a new heart, and without it he will die. Was I hearing things?" she asked fearfully.

"I know this news sounds bad, but many people have heart transplants nowadays and live very productive lives afterward," the nurse told Aniyah.

"What if he does not live long enough to find a heart?"

"We have to stay positive. Let's take this one day at a time, okay?"

"You're right, I'm sorry. It's just…"

"No, you have been through a lot, and I understand."

Aniyah had no idea how to handle such a situation; she'd never been faced with anything this horrific. It was all a bad dream that wouldn't end. She knew the next step was to call home and tell their families. Julian was never very close to his parents, but she had no idea how to break news like this to anyone. A trip to the priest's office later that night might be in order.

Aniyah grabbed her phone and sat down, and took a deep breath. The line rang. "Mom, it's Aniyah. I have some news about Julian. I don't know how to tell you, but he collapsed on our hike yesterday. They had to helicopter him to the hospital yesterday. Th-"

Julian's mother interrupted, "Wait! What do you mean he collapsed?"

"Yes, he has a heart defect from birth. It's not strong enough. The doctor said it's coronary artery disease. The heart muscle is weak and can't maintain his body anymore. We are adding him to the transplant list for a new one, but we don't know how long it will take. The doctor said with a new heart he should be alright and live a healthy life."

"And without?" her mother asked firmly.

"He will die, Mom," she replied.

"Die! What? There must be some mistake!"

"No, it's not a mistake or wrong diagnosis." The phone line went silent.

"Mom... are you still there?" Nothing. "Mom?" Silence... and then the phone went dead. Aniyah looked over at Julian and saw his head moving. "Julian, oh my God, Julian." She dropped the phone and ran to his side.

The nurses heard Aniyah shout and hurried to the room. "Welcome back, Julian. It's good to see you awake." He nodded in slow motion.

"Oh honey, it's so good to see you awake. I have been so worried. How do you feel?"

"Weak," he whispered.

"I know… but you'll be better soon, I promise." Aniyah needed to keep positive in front of her husband. She wanted to enjoy one night with him and keep the future at bay.

"Can I have some water?" he asked.

"Sure, baby, of course. Well… I have ice chips."

Julian nodded. "Yes." Over the next few hours he regained consciousness, and was able to communicate reasonably well.

The newlyweds spent one night together before reality bared its ugly head. Aniyah fought back the agony of tears as the hours passed. She felt guilty for wanting to spend one normal night with her husband; maybe it was selfish on her part, but she ignored the culpability. It would be the last time she knew Julian as the strong vibrant human being she loved.

She curled up on the tiny hospital bed next to her husband while they talked about their future through the night. Aniyah felt the warmth of his body next to hers, and listening to his heartbeat felt comfortable and secure. Reality forced both of them to face an unconscionable future, and she wanted to keep the horrifying truth hidden away forever.

"Aniyah…" Julian whispered. "Are you awake? The sun is coming up."

"Yes, baby."

"Can you open the blinds? I want to see the sunshine. After all, we are in Hawaii," he said hopefully.

"Sure, I'd be happy to."

"Oh, yes much better. Thank you."

"Are you…" she started to say.

"Oh, sorry. What time is the doctor coming? I need to get some answers."

"I know… let me go check." Aniyah didn't want to lie any longer, but telling him the truth was more than she could handle.

As Aniyah was leaving the room, Dr. McCarthy entered. A flood of emotion rushed through her body. The truth would not be contained any longer.

"Julian, I am Dr. McCarthy. I am glad to see you awake. I have gotten all your test results back and would like to review everything with you. Aniyah has been wonderful at keeping everyone informed. What I have to say might be distressing, but we must take it one day at a time."

Aniyah knew she had dodged a bullet when the doctor kept their conversation silent. "The results are not what I had hoped to see, but we have an option. You were born with a heart defect, something called coronary artery disease. If you are not familiar with the term, it's a weakening of the heart muscle. In this case, it's severe. The best option for a complete recovery is a heart transplant. Most patients live a normal, healthy life afterward. I have drawn up the paperwork to proceed if you both choose to do so. Do you want me to give you guys some time to discuss the outcome? It's a lot of information to process."

"Yes, please doctor. And thank you," Julian stated.

Aniyah sat in the chair with tears rolling down her cheeks. The situation overwhelmed every emotion in her body. It was something she could not contain any longer.

"Alright, I will finish my rounds and be back in a few hours. If you need me, please call one of the nurses and they can come and get me." They both nodded.

"Aniyah, did you know about this last night? I saw the doctor look at you several times."

She nodded, "Yes… but I just wanted to spend one more normal night with you before our world changed forever. Please forgive me, I am sorry."

"It's okay, I understand. You should have told me."

"I know…"

"Have you called my family?" he asked.

"I talked to my sister and your mom, but I did not know too much information. I told her we would call later."

"Good, thank you. The last thing I want to deal with is my mother right now." Aniyah looked at Julian in surprise. It was a side she'd never seen before.

"I want the transplant! I can't live like this, bedridden."

"I figured you would, so I asked them to get the paperwork started yesterday. We have to meet with the billing department this afternoon," she told him.

"It's going to be okay, promise. No matter what happens, remember I love you."

"I love you too! I am sorry for not telling you last night," she said with honest regret.

"I know… it's okay. We all make mistakes. You had a lot on your plate to deal with over the last few days. Go get the doctor, and let's get this going. Then maybe next week we can go home."

"Alright, I am ready to go home as well. I'll be right back."

The harsh reality of his situation left him silent. Shock took over, protecting his sanity. Julian couldn't believe his worst fears had come true; no matter how far you travel, the past will catch up sooner or later.

The doctor and Aniyah walked in a few minutes later. "Alright, Julian. Your wife says you want to move forward with the transplant, right?"

"Yes, that is right. But, when can I get out of here and go home?"

"Julian… I am afraid your heart condition is very serious, and we can't release you to fly anywhere. In fact, you will be moved to our long-term stay wing later today. Once the paperwork is finished, you will be moved to urgent status on the transplant list. The damage to your heart is irreversible and it will rapidly degrade. We need to keep you as calm and quiet as possible to minimize any risk of further complications."

The news left Julian speechless; it was the last thing he expected to hear. Suddenly, death stared him square in the face. Hope had been highjacked, leaving only despair. In a split second, his whole world shattered, leaving undiluted truth in the wake. His business, career, and future hung in the balance. He was stuck somewhere far from home, with maybe no possibility of going home again.

"Julian… Can you hear me?" Dr. McCarthy asked.

"Oh, yes, sorry. This is a lot to process, doc."

"I know. You guys take some time to talk. I will have billing come up with the pertinent papers to get this process started. Do you guys have any other questions for me right now?"

"No. Do you, Aniyah?" Julian asked.

"No."

"Thanks, doc."

"Absolutely, just take this one day at a time. I'll be back in the morning."

Aniyah and Julian sat in silence for some time. The recent turn of events left them searching for answers. Suddenly, their bright future faded quickly.

Julian knew he faced a daunting task telling his wife the truth about his past, something he never wanted to divulge. It was an event he had moved past many years ago, and he struggled daily to forget the images from his childhood. The fights with his parents, scuffles in school, girls that rolled through his life quickly, bad decisions… the list went on and on. He was embarrassed by his actions as an adolescent. His beautiful queen knew the person he was today, not the past.

"Aniyah, the last few days have brought up some events that are out of our control. I have faced some life and death situations in the past with my job, but this is the closest yet. Please, know that I love you with all of my heart. Now and forever. All I ever wanted for you was the best money could buy-"

"Julian… oh sorry- I don't care about your money. I married you because I love you. That's it! If we get rich together, so be it. If not, it's alright as well. The important thing is we live as one person. My heart belongs to you."

Julian lowered his head; it was time to face the truth and come clean. Aniyah deserved to know. "I have some things to tell you. They are awful and I am ashamed of my behavior, but not all the mistakes were my fault. Children cannot control the life their parents lead."

"Whatever you have to say, it won't change the way I feel about you, Julian."

"Thanks babe, but you might think differently when I tell you my story."

"Not going to happen! Do you hear me? We have been together a long time and I know the person you are inside. Do you think you are the only one who has regrets?"

"No, I guess not. But I need you to listen; hear me out, okay?"

"Yes, I will listen."

"Here it goes…. I am going to start with my parents. They had a strange marriage. I remember August 1984 the most vividly. We were evicted from our home; I don't know if my parents had money problems or not, but we relocated to the south side of Chicago where my grandmother lived. I was five at the time, and my life took a turn. My parents stayed married but never lived with each other. The whole thing seemed weird, but there were questions some five-year-old don't ask. They talked every day, so the reason is unknown. My dad worked north of us and literally lived at his job; I mean he slept in the dealership office or his car. He detailed vehicles at one of the local car dealerships. We always lived with Mom and were looked after by my grandmother. Dad was non-existent; he just provided for us financially.

"One afternoon Dad came to pick us up and said we would be staying with him for a few days. I got to see how my dad really lived. Mom was in the hospital having surgery, which meant he had to look after us for a short time. I still remember him pulling up in a van from the car lot and fixing up our beds in the back to sleep overnight. The next morning, we cleaned up in the dealership bathroom. We were shipped to a hotel the next day; maybe Dad got in trouble for having his kids there, I don't know. The reason my father lived at his work never really bothered me, I just figured it was because of the distance from our home.

"Mom did not work, as Dad said he vowed to care for us financially. Once I was an adult Mom started working, maybe she got tired of not having any money, I don't know.

"Things moved along for many years until my grandmother passed away from cancer when I was thirteen. She left the house to her four daughters. I never met my grandfather, because he passed before I was born. It wasn't until later I found out why Dad stayed away. He did not get along with my aunts. In any case, he was always there financially. Although I love my father dearly, I never forgot the night I saw him choking my mother. From that moment forward I know my life would be different..."

"Julian... I don't know what to say. Why didn't you tell me any of this stuff?"

"I was embarrassed. You have such a wonderful family. I was afraid if I told you the truth you'd leave."

"Leave! Is that what you think of me? Am I that shallow?"

"No... I'm sorry. I should have told you. Please forgive me?"

"I forgive you, I'm just upset that you hid this kind of information. Is that all?"

"Unfortunately, no. There is more a lot more." The room went silent. Aniyah stayed quiet.

"I'd like to tell you more, is that ok?" Aniyah nodded.

"The incident with my dad left me scarred, and I wanted to make a difference. So, the only option was to seek a career in law enforcement. The direction really didn't matter, whether it was a lawyer, correctional officer, or police officer. I just wanted to protect the innocent people who were unable to protect themselves."

Aniyah perked up at Julian's last statement.

"We lived on the south side of Chicago, a rough neighborhood with a lot of gang problems. Law enforcement was not always welcome, and many times I was quoted as saying I disliked the police because they would harass my friends and family as well as myself, but looking back now we probably deserved the questioning. However, I still felt that becoming a law enforcement officer would give me the opportunity to help the weak and innocent. The type of officer you become depends on your passion for the job.

"After I became an officer, my vision remained the same. We are out there to assist everyone we meet, whether it's from a casual conversation or chasing someone down bringing them to justice, doesn't matter. Aniyah you know me and who I am today. My job is to serve, to give back to the community and help the world become a better place, one citizen at a time."

Julian looked over at his wife, and the tears rolled down her cheeks. "Shall I continue?"

She choked out, "Yes."

"Growing up, our house was small, and Mom never had her own bedroom. She slept in a chair in the living room. My brother slept on the dining room floor under the table as there was nowhere else for him to sleep. Most people might wonder how any child can survive in these circumstances, but it gave me ambition to do better with my life.

"Once my siblings and I were old enough for school, my mother sent us to the same place she and her sisters went to school. Elementary school was a blur, however I remember sixth grade vividly. I was getting older and beginning to understand life; we walked home in a bad gang area that was known for selling drugs. My cousins were highly involved, and it put the same stigma on me. I struggled to stay away from the situation, but living among the predators and not falling prey was difficult.

"I believe my church-orientated family life helped save me from getting into too much trouble. As my mother was an evangelist, she had us in church faithfully every Sunday-"

"So… you did go to church. I did not know that about your mom."

"Yes, we did. And yes, I believe that saved me. Anyway, grade school is when I decided my pursuit of happiness would be in law enforcement. Without any tutoring, the right path remained silent. So, I chose my own path. It may not have been the best route, but I made it the best way I knew how.

"Julian… I'm going to head back to our hotel, take a shower and pack our things. I might as well check out and find something more affordable. Do you mind? Maybe I just need some alone time. Please don't be mad."

"Mad! How could I be upset with you for anything? You are my queen." Aniyah smiled, she liked the pet name. "Go do what you need. It's not like I'm going anywhere."

She chuckled, "I love you, Julian Parker." He nodded.

"I love you too. See you in a while."

"You can count on that. I'll be back as soon as possible."

The recent activity left Julian exhausted, but he did not want his wife to worry any more than she had already. The soft sound of him snoring could be heard a few minutes later.

Aniyah sat in the rental car, sobbing uncontrollably. The flow of emotions hit her hard. She fought to keep positive, but she knew the odds. In the hospital lobby was a pamphlet on heart transplants, and the statistics looked wonderful in the brochure. A Google search told a different story, one fact she vowed to keep silent. Julian had enough to deal with; he didn't need to worry about statistics.

Aniyah gathered herself and punched in the address to find the hotel. She was on autopilot. Numbness took over every inch of her soul. She repeated the silent prayers of hope diligently. It was the only thing that was keeping her sane, because Julian needed her to be strong.

Chapter Four:

Waiting

The night hours turned to early morning before either one of them stirred. Exhaustion had taken over and kept the couple in a deep sleep. Aniyah stirred. First, she looked up and saw Julian sleeping peacefully. If their time together was limited, she was going to take advantage of every second. But morning called and she had to sneak away to the bathroom. She gently moved his arm to crawl out of bed. Once clear, she rushed to the bathroom, but the swift movement caused blood to rush away from her head.

Suddenly, Aniyah felt dizzy and had to grab the chair for support. "Oh," she thought. "Wow."

Julian was still sleeping, and for that she was grateful. He needed the rest. While finishing her bathroom essentials, she heard the nurse enter to check morning vitals.

"Good morning, Julian. How are you feeling today?"

"I'm good. I feel much better after a good night's sleep."

"That is great. We are preparing your new room so the orderlies will be in soon to move you. We'll have your breakfast sent there."

"Sure, thanks," he replied.

Aniyah waited until the nurse left to reenter the room. She still was not eager to talk with anyone. "Morning, sweetheart. How are you?" Julian asked.

"I'm good."

"Are you sure? You look kind of pale."

"No, I'm ok really. Just hungry I guess," she replied.

"Why don't you go downstairs and get some breakfast? They are going to change all my bedding and get ready to move us anyway."

"Yeah, okay. Maybe I will. Good idea." Aniyah gave Julian a kiss and headed for the cafeteria.

The cool air-conditioned hallway felt cold against her skin. As the perspiration rushed down her body, she was forced to find a seat. Aniyah sat with her head between her knees, taking deep breaths. It took a few minutes, but the feeling passed. "I have to get some food in me," she thought.

The brief pause halted the dizziness, and she was able to get some breakfast. Aniyah ordered and found a table to sit. She liked having a view of the Hawaiian mountainside. It scared her to think of accepting the situation. It meant the outcome was real. Her coffee and scrambled eggs tasted good. "Maybe I was just hungry," she thought.

It was time to head upstairs and face Julian, the light of day and whatever else would be thrown at them today. Julian was in his new room when she got back from the cafeteria. She took a deep breath. "Hi, I'm back," she said cheerfully.

"Hey, honey. You look better. I see you got some food. Did you bring me a to-go bag?" He smiled.

"What do you want? I'll go get you something."

"I wish, but they have me on a special diet. I guess there are requirements for the transplant operation."

"Did they come to see you already?"

"Not, yet."

"I'm sorry… I should have been here."

"No… I did not mean that. You're fine. I know you needed some space, it's okay. You deserve that. Don't beat yourself up."

"Oh… Thank goodness. I felt really guilty for leaving for a while yesterday. I will go later this afternoon and find a place to stay. I found some reasonable apartments that rent on a month-to-month basis and some long stay motels. I can't believe we are talking about this kind of stuff. A few days ago, …"

"Honey, don't go there. It won't do either of us any good. We must deal with this; it's not going away. Please, don't worry. All it will do is make you sick." She nodded, Julian was right.

"I…"

"Sorry to interrupt. My name is Cassy, and I work in the billing and insurance department. I have all the paperwork ready for both of you to sign. Then we can determine what and if the insurance will cover the procedure. It will take a few days to get confirmation."

"Alright, so they may not cover the transplant?" Aniyah asked.

"No, it depends on the policy. They are all different."

"Well, I am a first responder," Julian stated.

"That's great. That will make it easier to get approved. Do you have any other questions to ask me?" Both parties shook their head no.

"Alright, then I will see you again when I have some information."

"Thank you, Cassy." Julian nodded.

"Well, that went pretty good, don't you think?" he asked.

"Yes, I guess. But, we are not yet approved."

"Think positive, babe! It will be okay." She agreed. The two chatted for some time, reminiscing. It felt good to just talk and not think.

"I better go, Julian. It's 2:30 p.m. and I want to get all this stuff done. We can at least have dinner together."

"Yes, go! Do what you must, but please be careful." Aniyah nodded and left in much better spirits.

Julian had never felt so helpless. In the past, he learned life has a way of turning the page when you least expect it. Sometimes, those changes leave unfinished business. He knew the time was coming for him to tell Aniyah about his past, no matter the outcome. He wanted so badly to call his family and have someone comfort him, but that would only lead to negative input.

A fateful statement rang in his head, as if it had been said yesterday, "I have no use for your excuses… if you acted like your brother and behaved, you might not have such problems. I gave up on you a long time ago. Everyone is right, you'll be nothing but a thug." His family's words sent chills up his spine.

The inclination to call home passed quickly. Besides, Aniyah had called home already. For a few moments, he was lost in the challenges of childhood. Children are born into a family and have no option to alter that outcome. After many years and the tribulations of life, you must *grow* through the changes.

Dr. McCarthy interrupted his reminiscing. "Good afternoon, Julian. How are you feeling today?"

"Doc... I feel great. Are you sure I must stay here? I don't feel out of breath or weak in any way."

"Okay, I will approve short outings on the hospital lawn. No more than once a day. But, you must ride in a wheelchair downstairs, and then you can walk outside to a table. Alright?"

"Oh, yeah, that is perfect! Doc I have spent the latter part of my life in the gym and exercising. It's killing me to just sit here and do nothing."

"Julian that is why you have stayed so healthy. It was your exercise routine that kept you alive this long," the doctor replied.

The news caught Julian off guard, learning that he had been living on borrowed time.

Aniyah had done some research on her phone to locate some options for apartments to rent. One caught her attention, "The original Hawaiian Inn." A local family had owned it for the last fifty years. They were close to the hospital and easy access, in a safe area of town. Sometimes, God just drives the car and you ride passenger.

As Aniyah drove into the parking lot, she felt comfortable. A home away from home. It was not a brand-new business with all the premium luxuries, but good atmosphere is always preferable.

"Hello, how can I help you?" the desk clerk asked.

"Hi, I need to rent a long-term stay room, please."

"Sure, with one bed or two? Queen or king?" she asked.

"One queen bed. It will be just for me right now. My husband is in the hospital, and we are here for an extended stay," she replied.

"I am sorry, we'll keep you in our prayers. Is it serious, if you don't mind me asking?"

"No… not at all. Yes, he is waiting on a heart transplant. We came on our honeymoon and found out he has a heart defect. The only option is a transplant to save his life. Our doctor won't release him to fly home."

"Oh my! Honey, that is awful. On your honeymoon no less. I have our best room open, you can have that one."

"Thank you… I probably won't be here that much, but whatever you have is great."

"Come on, I'll show you the way and get you settled in." They walked in silence.

"Here we are, I hope this works for you?"

"I'm sure it will. Thank you again."

"It's my pleasure. If there's anything we can do, please come ask." Aniyah nodded her head.

The only thing on her mind was making sure Julian had everything he needed. She settled in, putting some clothes in the dresser, and filling the refrigerator with the items she grabbed at the store. It was far from home, but it was a roof over her head.

Aniyah decided to take a bath and clean up before heading back to the hospital. She would be there most, if not all, of the night. The hot water gave instant relief to her aching muscles and head. She'd felt off since yesterday, and her stomach had been doing somersaults all day. While in the grocery store the smell of the seafood deli made her want to vomit. She had to choke back the feeling. But Julian had enough on his plate to worry about; he didn't need this added to the menu.

Julian paced the floor in his mind out of boredom. He'd never sat in one place for so long. It was excruciating, and being alone in that hospital compounded his agony. He missed Aniyah; she had a way of calming his fears.

It's difficult to keep occupied when you're sitting in a hospital bed, void of any activities. He had called his partner to send a laptop so he could at least help with the paperwork and affairs that pertained to running the business. He decided to text his wife and make sure she was alright.

"Hi honey, how's it going?" he texted.

Aniyah had left the phone in the other room while taking a bath, so she missed his text. The hot bathwater washed away all her congestion from being stuck so far from home. She had always been close to her family and missed them terribly.

Julian waited impatiently, fearing the worst. He texted several more times, "Aniyah, everything all right? I'm getting worried."

Once she got out of the tub, she heard the alert on her phone. She rushed to check; there were six texts from Julian, "Honey, w r u?"

"Sorry, I found a place and took a bath before coming back to the hospital. I am bringing my dinner with me, be back soon. Love you!" she texted back. He took a sigh of relief.

Julian was eager to take a walk outside, feel the warm ocean breeze on his skin, smell the flowers blooming and just be a part of society once again. He had a whole new understanding of people who were bedridden or homebound. The news he could go outside brought some joy to an otherwise tumultuous situation. He thought, "Maybe if I imagine myself in the gym working out it will have an effect on my body." Anyway, it was something to pass the time.

The sun was resting low on the horizon before Aniyah got back from the new apartment. "Hi, baby! I am sorry for taking so long. It was a grueling afternoon. I checked about six places and ended up just down the street about ten minutes away. It takes longer to drive and park the car than walk. How are you feeling?" she asked.

"I am doing better. The doctor says we can go outside on the hospital lawn. I need to get out of this room for a while. Please? This is driving me crazy."

"OMG! Really? That's fantastic. Let's go!" she told him.

"The orderly will be back soon, I told them you were on your way back. I have to ride in a wheelchair downstairs."

"At least we can get you out of here even for a short time."

Aniyah told Julian about the place she found while they waited for the orderly. It was her choice since he was stuck in the hospital. The newlyweds were adjusting to their situation; fighting it was pointless. Hope remained the only recourse.

Chapter Five:

Ocean Breeze

Julian and his bride made their way outside to the hospital lawn. The warm ocean breeze caressed his face. He could feel the sun teasing his skin as he walked to the picnic table. Julian felt alive for the first time in his life. Death has a way of changing the way we face the world.

"Aniyah, I never imagined just going outside could bring so much joy."

"I can see why you feel that way. You've been locked up inside for days, and you are used to being outside working and staying active every day. I feel helpless, Julian. There is nothing I can do to change what's happening."

"I know, babe. This is a nightmare that won't end. Well, I guess that's not true. If I d-"

"Don't even think like that, do you hear me?" she demanded.

"You're right, I'm sorry."

Aniyah smiled at Julian. "Come on… sit with me, and we can watch the sunset."

The two sat in silence, watching the magnificent scenery casting its beauty across the sky. Julian's mind wandered to how his wife had processed his confession. She'd been quiet about the information since they talked the night before.

"An-" Julian started to say.

"Jul- I'm sorry. Go ahead," she told him.

"No…. please. What were you going to say?"

"Please continue with what you wanted to tell me last night. It's not dark yet, so go ahead. I'm listening."

"Are you sure?" She nodded. Aniyah wanted to get this over with; the suspense was awful.

"I know now… all my choices weren't perfect, and I made some dumb decisions, but we must proceed with the hand we're dealt. The trick is manipulating the hand to work in your best interests. I don't mean violence or anything illegal. We all have a brain and the choice of whether to use it depends on the person. The lessons in life are demanding and it's normal to make mistakes; life is an experience. Our objective is to learn from those mishaps and go forth with a better understanding. Do you understand my frame of mind better?"

"Yes, that helps a lot. Keep going," she told Julian.

"Okay, here it goes. Sixth grade ended being the most challenging. I think that's the age our brain learns the meaning of reason. Our clarity opens, and we see things as they really are for the first time. We start to build personalities, likes and dislikes. Adulthood thrives, and we gain independence in our home life and at school. The teachers give us choices, and we can finally decide for ourselves.

"I think this is when the issues really began. At the beginning of school, I lost my front tooth. My courage fell through the floor. My mother tried to tell me multiple times, it's only temporary. The new tooth will grow in, but to a sixth grader, two weeks is like an eternity. Since my self-esteem was already low, I became a small fish in a big pond. I struggled to fit in somewhere.

"Gang life seemed more appealing every day. In my mind, at least, they wanted me to be a part of their family. In the beginning, there would be concessions, but they were only temporary. Once that was over, I would not be asked to repeat any actions. I could feel important.

"My mind was made up, and it seemed an appealing decision at the time. I headed to meet up with my cousin, and took a shortcut down an alley. But then I witnessed something that would forever alter the course of my life. Two gang members were beating up a young kid behind some old buildings. The kid was screaming for help, and I could see the other members across the street laughing at someone else's pain. A gut-wrenching agony took over and I knew my decision would lead me to a place that there was no coming back from. I do believe God was working on my conscience that day.

"I feel bad for not coming to that kid's rescue, but I was one person against many other kids. So instead, I ran for the nearest phone and called for help. I found out later the young boy was alright physically, but I am sure he ended up with some emotional scars. Avoiding gang life was one of the best decisions I ever made, although my life did not get any easier after this difficult choice. In many ways, it got worse."

"Okay, so you stayed out of a gang. What happened after that?"

"I'm getting to that part. One afternoon, just before lunch, several us of decided to skip math class and mess around. We hung out behind the gymnasium, and one of the kids saw DeShawn entering the bathroom. He was especially disliked by his fellow classmates. I really didn't have an opinion either way, but they tried to force me into showing my worth. Since I did not join the gang, they increased the pressure.

"Several of us took off and chose not to be a part of their bad behavior. What I didn't know was, the two kids who stayed went in the bathroom and proceeded to beat the tar out of DeShawn. A few minutes later, my English teacher heard the commotion and came to break up the fight, but the kids took off before Mr. Remold could catch them in the act. Needless to say, he was well versed in fight situations and did not tolerate such actions by anyone. When he questioned them, they spilled the beans, blaming me. The bullies were just innocent bystanders and ran to avoid getting in trouble for being in the bathroom. I was suspended for two weeks, paired with a warning about my behavior. When I tried to proclaim my innocence, I was told that lying was bad form and advised to straighten up."

Aniyah sighed.

"My mother apparently did not approve of the actions and immediately called my father. I got way more than just a suspension from school. Dad never hit us kids, but his lecture was enough to scare me for a short time. I spent the remainder of my suspension in detention at home.

"At first, the incident made me look good at school with the girls, but with my low self-esteem the popularity did not last long. The combination of my poor self-image and dark complexion meant the girls made fun of me. I was angry for being blamed for something I had not done. When I tried to confess my innocence, it had the opposite effect. No one believed me, and the only thing that suffered was my grades. My life continued to spiral downward quickly."

"Julian… I had no idea you went through all this stuff."

"No, no one does. I got very good at hiding the hurt. One Friday night shortly after I returned to school from my suspension, I felt just about as low as any person could handle. My mom came home from work, and I asked if we could talk. I was seeking comfort from a parent. She looked disgusted at my request but obliged.

"We sat down at the kitchen table with the family lurking to oversee my questions. Let's just say the result was anything than what I expected.

"I remember the conversation vividly, as if it happened yesterday. I said, 'Mom, I'm really struggling in school. I don't have any friends, girl or boy, that treat me like a person. The girls relentlessly make fun of me and then get their so-called boyfriends to teach me a lesson. When I fight back, I am the one who gets in trouble. Yeah, I hang with the wrong crowd to keep safe; it's the only way. I don't know what to do.'

"Her response was anything but maternal. 'You are full of justification, aren't you? Maybe if you altered your behavior these things might stop happening. It's not just about you. I gave up on you a long time ago. Everyone one is right, you'll be nothing but a thug.' Her words sank deep, I was mortified."

"WAIT! Your mother told you that stuff? You were just a kid. I can't imagine anyone in my family ever saying anything like that to me," Aniyah blurted out.

"She chased me out of the kitchen and told me to go to my room. Depression set in, uncontrollable sadness. The confrontation left me heartbroken. How could my mother say such horrible things about her child? No matter what happened, no kid deserves to hear those kinds of things from their parents. It almost took my will to live, but something inside drove me to keep going, no matter how things looked at the moment. I wondered if life was worth living, but we all have a purpose, and mine was to fight and live another day."

The sky darkened, but Aniyah was hooked. She needed to hear the rest.

"I decided to join the basketball team. I thought the exercise and athletic challenge might help my situation. My self-esteem did improve, but I continued to fight every day. The battle raged on throughout the year, and my grades continued to slide.

"In the afternoons, I went with my mom to the grocery store and would always steal candy. One day I was caught by security and asked to never return to that store. My mom was so embarrassed. At the time, it was the actions of a sixth grader seeking attention. I feel bad for the problems I caused. However, the stealing didn't end there; not too long after the grocery store incident I stole 100 dollars from my grandmother's purse. Then to top off the year, I failed the sixth grade."

"You…. failed sixth grade? No, I can't believe that."

"It's true. But, I made myself a promise to never fail anything again. During the summer, a childhood friend was killed due to gang involvement. It further engrained my decision to never give up without a fight. The best thing about my sixth-grade year was I learned to focus. I developed character and the ambition to make something of myself with what life provided.

"During the last week of school, we always had field day, and for the first time in my life, I won a high jumping contest. I have always been a good athlete but never had the confidence to pursue winning. But, most importantly, I finally passed the sixth grade."

"I am speechless. You are so different, it's hard to think of you as insecure," she said.

"I was, believe it or not, and maybe even still am to this day. I mean, that's why I was afraid to tell you the truth. For the better part of my youth, people always told me what a screw up I was and I'd never become anything important. After a while, you start to believe the garbage. It becomes a part of your soul, and it creates the person you become. This is why I told you my faith and church life have kept me pressing forward, no matter what happens. Am I making any sense?"

"Yep, you are. I am beginning to understand why you stay away from your family. I always thought something was amiss, but you just confirmed my suspicions. I don't think I would have been so forgiving of my family under these circumstances. I give you credit for trying to remain a respectful."

"Thank you. I wish we would have had this conversation in the beginning. It would have saved me a lot of turmoil."

"I agree, and I'm not happy you have kept this a secret. It's upsetting you didn't trust me enough to tell the truth. Besides, if I had left or gotten mad, would you really have wanted me around?" Aniyah asked.

"No, I suppose not. Thanks, babe, for listening. I feel much better. Although there is more to say, we can talk more tomorrow. Are you ready to go back to the room? All this fresh air has me drained," he said.

"Okay, I'll get the wheelchair." She walked away feeling relieved.

Julian knew he had dodged a bullet. God brought him an extraordinary person to share his life with, and he could not hide secrets any longer. Life lesson learned, always tell the truth.

"Come on honey, get in." Julian rolled his eyes; riding in a wheelchair was embarrassing. Although, under the circumstances, it could get worse quickly.

"Honey, thank you for finally being honest and telling me the truth. I love you," Aniyah told him.

Julian turned his head and smiled. He felt like a huge weight had been lifted off his shoulders. It was a positive ending to a negative situation. The two made their way back to the room in silence.

"Julian… after we eat, I'm going to go take a shower and get some clean clothes, okay?"

"Absolutely, I understand. Besides, the nurses will be in to change the sheets and help me shower, anyway. So, take the time you need. Call your family and check in. Send them my love, alright?"

"I will." The dinner tray was waiting in Julian's room when they returned.

Julian struggled with moving around too much, he was getting weak quickly. It broke Aniyah's heart to see him in this situation, but she tried to direct the conversation to the lighter side of life. "Looks like they brought our dinner."

"Yeah… would you like to trade? My beef broth looks yummy."

"No, I'll pass. But here, sneak a bit of my chicken."

"Oh, God that is good. Thank you." Julian accepted the situation, knowing full well his future was in the hands of fate.

Aniyah felt a sense of relief after hearing the truth. She had always felt the tension with Julian's family. But she was still disappointed by his actions.

The hotel room felt like a sanctuary in a world filled with chaos. Aniyah had always been close to her family, and this experience made her realize how truly blessed she was for having a stable childhood.

As she walked into the room her phone rang, "Hello?" The dark room made it impossible to see the caller ID. She panicked every time someone called these days.

"Hi sis! How are you today? Is Julian alright? I have not heard anything for a while."

"Sofia… I am so glad you called. I miss you."

"I know, honey, me too. I thought maybe I could fly in to see you in the next few weeks. I'll try to get some time off work."

"Oh my God, really??? I would love that."

"Okay, I'll let you know. Now, are you alright? You sound sad."

"I am… all this mess, it's so hard. But, then Julian confessed his past tonight."

"His past? What past…?"

"You know he has never really talked about his family or sees them, but now I know why. It was a bad situation. I am upset he kept this from me for so long. I mean, if this hadn't happened, I may have never found out the truth."

"What do you mean, bad situation?"

"Their living arrangements were weird, and his dad was only around to provide financial support. Well, other than trying to choke his mom once. Then, in sixth grade he almost joined a gang, but-"

"WAIT! He was in a gang?" Sofia shouted.

"NO! I said 'almost'."

"Okay, that's a relief. Go on…"

"Well, he saw the gang members beating up a young kid, and he got scared. Julian took off before they saw him."

"What about the kid? Did he not help them?"

"No, there were too many of them, so he ran to a phone and called for help. The kid was okay, just beat up and bruised." Aniyah told her.

"Is that all he told you?" Sofia asked.

"There is more, but it was late and I needed a break to catch my breath. This has been a lot to handle over the last week. I mean, we don't even know if the insurance will cover the operation. I am trying to stay calm and take this one day at a time, sis. I-"

Sofia interrupted, "Sis, everything will be okay, promise. Just have faith. We may not be there in person, but we are always there in spirit."

"Thank you, Sofia. I can't imagine not having you as my strength. Poor Julian he has no one."

"That's not true, he has you!" Aniya felt the love in her sister's affirmation.

"Well, sis, I am going to take a bath and head back to the hospital. I love you."

"I love you too. Please give Julian my love. Tell him I am always here if he needs to talk."

"I will. Bye. Talk tomorrow," Aniyah stated.

"Bye."

Julian waited patiently for his bride to return. The nurses had changed his bedding, and he got to take a shower for the first time in a week. Sponge baths are for the birds.

Aniyah wanted so badly for this nightmare to end; she refused to accept her husband dying. If he couldn't fight, she'd fight for him. It's amazing how bath and clean clothes can lift your spirits. A quick stop for coffee and she was back at the hospital. It had been a few weeks since she'd had a caramel macchiato.

Julian heard his wife's voice coming down the hallway. She was always pleasant with the hospital staff. Just knowing Aniyah was close made his trepidations fade.

"Hi babe, glad you're back," Julian told her.

"Hi! How are you feeling?"

"Better. I got to take a shower by myself. It was marvelous."

"I can imagine, and I thought it smelled better in here," she stated in jest.

"Ha ha! Come over here," Julian requested. Aniyah snuggled in next to her husband. It felt good to just lie down in his strong arms.

"Good night babe! Sleep well," Julian whispered. Aniyah was already asleep. He kissed her forehead, "I love you, my bride."

His thoughts ran rampant, and Julian knew he had to confess everything. He needed to come clean while he still had time. Time was something he never gave much thought to until this last week. It's amazing, how one incident can alter one's reality forever.

It was almost one a.m. before Julian finally fell asleep. He tried to watch some nonsense on cable, an attempted distraction. Unfortunately, nothing worked; death has a way of halting all life's plans. The nurse's advice was correct: "Take it one day at a time."

Aniyah gradually stirred as the morning lit up the room with a gentle glow. She was grateful to be alive and spend one more day with Julian. She eased off the bed and headed for the bathroom. She bumped into the wall; something was wrong. It was the second morning she felt nauseous.

Her mind raced, "Did I eat last night? Was it the coffee?" Nothing fit the scenario.

She made her way into the bathroom and tried to stabilize her stomach. The cold floor felt good. A few minutes later, she heard the nurse enter Julian's room. Aniyah tried to stand, but it took everything she had to keep from throwing up. The blood rushed from her head, and she broke out into a cold sweat. "Oh…" she thought.

Aniyah sat on the floor and listened to the nurse and Julian chat about his vital signs. She struggled to regain composure while they talked. "How's Aniyah this morning?" the nurse asked.

"Good, I guess. She was already awake when you came in."

"Okay, well if you need anything else just call."

Julian nodded, "Yes."

A few minutes later, Aniyah came out of the bathroom. The nauseous feeling had passed. "Good morning honey, are you okay? You don't look so good."

"Yes, I am alright. Why do you ask?" she asked.

"You look kind of green around the gills."

"Oh… I feel queasy this morning."

"You were sick yesterday morning, but I saw you eat last night. Maybe the doctor should check you out."

"No… no, I am fine. It's just been a long few days," she replied.

"Honey, I think-"

The doctor entered the room and interrupted, "Good morning, Julian. How are you feeling?"

"I am good doc, but my wife is not feeling so well." Aniyah looked at him, disgusted.

"Really, I am fine," she told him.

"You don't look so fine. Sit down, let me take a look."

Aniyah sat down. "When did this start?"

"A few days ago. My stomach has felt upset, but only in the mornings."

"In the mornings?" he asked.

"Yes. Why, what's wrong?"

"Nothing's wrong, I'd say you are pregnant. I can't say without a test, but that is my guess."

"WHAT! I'm pregnant?" she exclaimed.

"Doc, did you say she is pregnant?"

"I can't say for sure without testing, but yes. Let me get the nurse and we'll take you downstairs."

Aniyah sat speechless; it was the last thing she ever expected. "Babe…that is fantastic! The best news we've had since this whole mess started."

She turned to Julian, "We don't know for sure yet."

"I do!" he stated firmly.

Chapter Six:

The Final Results

Life changes lanes when you least expect it. Aniyah and Julian found out they were having their first child. It was a sweet reward from the genuine love they shared.

Aniyah sat in the waiting room for the final results. The shock had finally worn off, and she was able to process the information. It was something they had discussed many times, and both of them wanted children once they had been married for a while and settled down. Although, as they both learned, some things are out of your control. The best course of action was to accept the changes and adopt an optimistic outlook.

The nurse came into the waiting room, "Aniyah... can you come with me?" She nodded. As they walked down the long hallway, her heart raced. She had accepted things and prayed the results were positive.

She followed the nurse into the doctor's office. "You can have a seat, he'll be in shortly."

"Thanks," she replied.

Aniyah looked around at the family pictures on the desk, artwork on the wall and the general feel of the doctor's office. It was difficult to sit and wait; her nerves were frazzled.

"Hi, Aniyah. I am Dr. Waters. Well, Dr. McCarthy was right, you are pregnant; eleven weeks. I ran your blood work and everything looks great. I will write you a prescription for prenatal vitamins. If you could call my office, I'd like to see you in the next couple of weeks for a complete checkup."

Aniyah stared at the doctor, and all she could do was nod. Their dream of having a baby was real, not just a suspicion. "Thank you," she managed to say.

"You're welcome. I know about your husband. I am not a heart surgeon, but his odds are excellent. If you need anything else, let me know. Oh… I also added a prescription for your morning sickness. It should help, but if not, we'll try something else. That should pass over the next month."

"Alright, thanks again," she replied. Joy filled her soul; the relief was overwhelming. Aniyah bounced upstairs. She couldn't wait to tell Julian it was official. The news would brighten both their spirits and give them hope for a bright future.

Julian waited anxiously for his wife's return. The nurses even looked curious when she walked back into the transplant ward. "Well?" one nurse asked.

She smiled and nodded. They cheered. Julian heard the commotion and knew his hunch was correct.

Aniyah's glow filled the room when she entered. "Babe! This is fantastic. I am so excited."

"It's amazing," she replied. Both were aware of the underlying circumstances, but at this moment neither one cared. They wanted to bask in the glow of a new life being created,

Chapter Seven:

New Life

For the next twenty-four hours, joy overtook them. Aniyah and Julian celebrated their incredible news. It was as if Julian's heart condition didn't exist. They wanted to drag out the experience indefinitely.

In the midst of the chaos, something always comes along to alter the outcome; the newlyweds had learned the meaning of this clearly over the last month. It's an unsettling thought that life is created from death. But, the reality is not always pleasant. Truth itself is difficult to digest.

Aniyah spent the night in the hospital once again; it was the only place she could find peace in this unfamiliar land. The medicine the doctor prescribed worked, and she was almost back to feeling normal. On her way back to the hospital, she stopped at the local bookstore to buy the book, "What to Expect When You're Expecting." Her sister recommended it as a good read. As a new mother, Aniyah wanted to be well-informed. Nothing perturbed her more than being left in the dark. It was the one lingering irritation she had with Julian for not being honest upfront.

The image of a hospital as her new home kept her feeling anxious. It was hard to relax when your loved one is facing the idea of death at a young age. Aniyah struggled each day to keep her mind on positive things and avoid the lingering situation. On her way upstairs to the ICU, the code alarms were ringing loudly and her heart leaped. The panic settled deep as she rushed through the corridor, praying it was not her husband. Julian was in room 3321, down the hall, last room on the left. She knew it by heart.

Aniyah saw Dr. McCarthy dash past her in a flash, and she froze. The only sound she could hear was her heart pounding. It was deafening. Why had she left? She should have come back faster; the book was not necessary.

Suddenly a nurse grabbed her shoulders. "Aniyah, come with me please."

The contact startled her and she jumped, "Oh!"

"I'm sorry. Please… come with me."

Aniyah followed her in silence. She felt the weight of her situation causing her knees to collapse. The nurse grabbed her quickly as they rushed to the waiting room.

"Aniyah… Aniyah can you hear me?" she heard a voice say.

The words rang clear, but nothing registered. She could not respond. "Aniyah, it's Dr. McCarthy. Can you hear me?"

Finally, things started to clear as reality took hold, and she nodded. "Yes, I can hear you."

"Good, don't try to sit up. Just listen. Julian went into cardiac arrest. We were able to get him stable, but his situation is not good. Right now, he's on heavy sedation. You won't be able to talk with him for a while. I'm hoping to get him stable again. But, he will be on oxygen full-time. When you are ready, the registration department needs to meet with you," Dr. McCarthy advised.

Aniyah sputtered, "What do they want?"

"I don't know. You will have to speak with them." Aniyah nodded.

"Great. I'll check on you again later," Dr. McCarthy stated.

The words registration department made things seem too real. "Hi, Aniyah. My name is Suzie. I have been assigned to your case. How are you doing? I am sorry; I can't imagine what you must be going through."

Aniyah nodded. Talking with anyone was the last thing on her mind. "What do you need?"

"I will make this speedy. Your insurance company is refusing to pay for the transplant. I requested to have Dr. McCarthy write a letter of recommendation to them, as per why Julian is a good candidate. We are hoping that will persuade them to change their minds. They were ordering Julian be released today, but the current situation will force them to let him stay until he is stable. I have put together some options, foundations that will take cases like Julian's. It's a long shot but worth a try. In this folder is all their contact information. I would like to take care of this right away. The faster you can get approval the better. Until you have coverage, Julian will be taken off the transplant list. I am sorry, there is nothing I can do. Do you have any questions?"

The words ceased to have any meaning, nothing made sense. "Why pay and have all this insurance if you can't use it when needed?" she wondered. It was not Suzie's fault, and the last thing Aniyah wanted to do was take her anger out on an innocent person.

"No…" she shook her head. "Thank you. I'll get right on calling these places."

Aniyah sat on the couch in complete dismay. "How much worse can this get?" she thought. Then, reality hit. Julian could di-. She choked on the words. In light of this new information, she formulated a plan. It was time to get serious and find someone willing to pay for her husband's transplant. The last thing she wanted to do was leave the hospital, but to have some peace and quiet she had to head to the hotel. Aniyah checked with the nurse on duty before she left. Seeing him in that bed broke her heart; there lay her life. She prayed.

It was difficult containing her composure while exiting the hospital, but it was necessary. She needed the security of her car before she could break down. Aniyah sat sobbing uncontrollably in the front seat. Life is completely unpredictable; one minute you're floating along on cloud nine and the next you are lying in a sewer ditch somewhere.

Then, something struck a nerve to bring her back to reality. Suddenly, she remembered the baby, an entity developing inside her body. The thought gave her comfort; she wasn't alone anymore. Her weeping stopped, and an unknown force took over. She felt refreshed. A driving notion implored her to press forward.

Aniyah spent the afternoon calling each foundation asking for help, each one responding with "I wish there were something we could do…"

It was frustrating, but nothing would stop her from finding a benefactor.

During her phone calls, the maid came by to clean and drop off new linens, Aniyah asked them to come back later. When her calls were finished, she walked to the office to inform them the maid could come back at any time.

As she stood there, the stress enveloped her body. "Aniyah it's so nice to see you, dear. How are you?" the owner asked.

A sudden breakdown came over her, and she began to sob again. "Julian is worse. He went into cardiac arrest this morning, and the doctors don't know how much longer he has. Plus, the insurance is refusing to pay for the transplant.

I don't know what do to. I've called every foundation on the list they gave me, but no one will commit."

"Oh... honey, I am so sorry. I may have an idea." Aniyah's eyes lit up.

"Really? Anything!"

"I have a friend over at St. Joseph's. He may be able to help."

"What is St. Joseph's?"

"They are a research hospital and offer free services to many people under the right circumstances. I think your situation might apply. Let me call him while you here."

"Oh my God! I would be forever grateful."

Aniyah waited patiently during the phone call. An appointment was scheduled for that afternoon at two o'clock. "I don't know how to thank you!"

"You already have; your tender care is enough. I can only hope you will return the favor to someone else one day."

"I will! Thank you." Aniyah rushed back to her room so she could shower and clean up before the meeting.

Upon entering the room her phone beeped, an alert to a voice mail. Her heart stopped once again. "Oh my God!" she thought.

The message was from her husband's business partner. Since Julian had been gone for the last month, they were not able to deposit a paycheck this week. When he was back and could contribute again, they would proceed with sending money. Julian's disability would not kick in for thirty days. They were hoping to live on Julian's paycheck this month. Aniyah wanted to falter; the issue was serious, but not life-threatening. She had to stay focused and resolve this insurance problem, or nothing else would matter anyway. Aniyah grabbed the doorknob, took a deep breath, and prepped herself for the meeting.

She was grateful to have a GPS to navigate around an unfamiliar city. The closer she got to the destination, the more her stomach turned. It was the last chance she had to save her husband's life.

"Hi, I have an appointment with Adam Bancroft at two o'clock."

"Okay, thank you. If you could have a seat, he'll be with you shortly." Aniyah nodded.

She sat down and looked around the office at pictures of grateful patients, awards, and such. On the coffee table were pamphlets about the organization. One brochure in particular caught her eye; it was about family assistance. The foundation paid living expenses for immediate loved ones so they could be close by the patient. Already, things looked brighter.

"Aniyah?" Adam asked.

"Yes," she replied.

"Please, right this way." He held the door open to his office. "Have a seat."

"Thank you."

"Now, I hear your husband is in the hospital and needs to have a heart transplant, but your insurance is refusing to cover the cost, is that right?"

"Yes, they will be releasing him as soon as he is stable again."

"What do you mean stable again?" Adam asked.

"He went into cardiac arrest this morning, and the doctors said he does not have much longer to live. They pulled him from the transplant list when the insurance refused to cover the cost. Plus, they will no longer cover his stay. I don't know what to do. And, I just found out I am pregnant. Our first child. We were visiting on our honeymoon when this happened."

"Oh, my! Well, congratulations, to start. I'd like to ask some questions first. What does your husband do for a living?"

"He is a correctional officer. Plus, he just started a business, sports attire. He also volunteers and works with troubled teens in Chicago, where we are from."

"A first responder, perfect! I can help for sure. One of our primary associations deals with helping first responders. I will have to get some paperwork filled out and make a few phone calls to verify everything, but we'll have you set up by next week. In the meantime, we will get him back on the transplant list and moved to our facility."

Aniyah sat in the chair as tears flowed down her cheeks. She was utterly speechless. "Yes," she nodded. "Alright, but what about me? We have no other income right now. Julian's disability from the city will not pay out for 30 days. His boss started the paperwork."

"Good, I'm glad you told me that. I will get you set up with housing. We don't cover personal expenses but we can cover living costs."

"No problem, I can get by for a month."

"Okay, do you have any other questions right now?" Adam asked.

"No, I don't think so," she replied.

"Here is my number if you think of something. I will be contacting the hospital tomorrow and arranging to have Julian moved. In the meantime, relax. You are in good hands." The words of an angel sounded loud and clear.

The meeting went better than she expected, and a weight had been lifted from her shoulders. Aniyah could finally breathe. Now Julian just had to hang on long enough for a viable transplant. She ran into the deli next door to get a sandwich and head back to the hospital. It was a blessing no one called from the ICU.

As Aniyah stepped out of the business complex into the warm sunshine, she could feel the rays caressing her skin. It had been weeks since she felt the sting of summer sun on her face. A break was in order, and the tables outside the sandwich shop called her name. Some fresh air was just what the doctor ordered. Julian would never want her to skimp on health for any reason. She sat admiring the beautiful scenery. Hawaii was an incredible place, but she missed Chicago.

"Can I get you anything else?" a waiter asked.

"No, I am good. Thank you," she replied.

While she sat admiring the view, it was the first time since all this started that Aniyah felt calm. Somehow, she knew deep down that Julian would live. It was a comforting thought.

As she finished her sandwich, the ocean beach called her name. It was an alluring presence she wanted desperately to enjoy. Although, telling Julian the great news was of the utmost importance.

Aniyah entered the ICU ward filled with apprehension, praying for the best. "Hi, how is Julian doing?" she asked the nurse on duty.

"So, far he's stable. A good sign. I think the doctor is in with him right now."

"Great!" she dashed towards his room. "Hi, doc, how is he?" she asked hopefully.

"His vitals are stable. I am glad to see him holding steady. But, how are you? Feeling alright?"

"Yes, much better. The medication for my morning sickness is working. Otherwise, I feel fine."

"Did you get a chance to tell Julian before this last episode?"

"I did, and he is very excited. Maybe it will be an extra boost for him to hang on.'

"I agree. If you need anything, let me know," he stated.

"Yes, thank you."

In the excitement, she forgot to tell the doctor about her good news. "Julian, I don't know if you can hear me, but we have insurance to cover your surgery. They will be moving you tomorrow, plus I will have housing while we are here in Hawaii. Please, baby, hang on. I need you. Please don't leave me!" she sobbed. Julian squeezed her hand, and she glanced up. He looked at her and smiled. "Baby, you're awake?"

Julian was incoherent but acknowledged her statement. "It's going to be okay, I promise," she told him.

The stress of the day hit Aniyah hard, and standing or acknowledging anyone was unimaginable. She moved to the small couch and collapsed.

Chapter Eight:

Things Happen for a Reason

Julian was moved to the new facility but remained in critical condition. Housing was established for Aniyah, a small apartment that was adequate since she spent most of her time at the hospital. The impending doom was on both their minds. Julian's situation continued to worsen as the days passed. He remained on oxygen full-time and was remanded to his bed. Any extra stress on his heart could be fatal. They prayed for a miracle.

Since the move to the new hospital, several months had passed and Aniyah started to show. Her pregnancy was progressing nicely. Under the circumstances, the staff arranged to have her ultra-sounds in Julian's room. It was most definitely the highlight of his life.

Aniyah took a job at the local coffee shop down the street from her apartment. It was a close walk, so she was able to return the rental car. If she had to travel around the island, she took a taxi. The rates were cheaper than paying for a rental car. She worked the late afternoon shift since Julian slept most of the day; mornings seemed to be his best time. It gave her time to go home and shower before breakfast, spend some time with Julian, and kept her busy in the afternoon before dinner. Her only expenses were food and personal items. Julian and his business partner agreed to a compromise; they covered all of Aniyah and Julian's living expenses in Chicago, and in return he did not take a salary.

Aniyah had met several other people they shared a bond with: family members with loved ones waiting on the transplant list. It gave her a sense of closeness and support. Plus, with her pregnancy, she never felt alone anymore. The baby served as a companion. She spent many hours talking to her fetus.

The past, however, constantly reappeared. Julian was insistent on confessing his transgressions before anything serious happened. Despite Aniyah's objections, Julian felt it was imperative.

"Aniyah, please, I have to get this stuff off my chest. You are the only one I trust."

"I know, Julian, but just know it's not necessary. I love you no matter what happened in your past. It's not where you came from, it's where you are going. The man before me is brilliant. Honorable to a fault."

The words hit Julian hard; he'd never heard his wife be so honest and upfront with her feelings. It was refreshing. Aniyah was never dishonest; she just kept her thoughts to herself most times. It was important to her to respect other people's feelings.

"After I failed the sixth grade, my confidence fell beyond belief. I felt like such a failure and contemplated suicide, but fortunately my brother saved me from making such a fatal decision. When we get older age doesn't play a big factor, but in school, it's a different story. Although I faced the kids who relentlessly made fun of me, it was watching my friends move to the front and leaving me in the rear that hurt the worst. I just was not willing to face facts; my failures were the cause of everything."

"I hope you weren't the only one," Aniyah said.

"Yes, a few friends who went through the sixth grade failed as well, so we were all redoing it again. But, I found out that some of them were leaving class early to have an extra gym period, take exams outside of class, and were given extra help and tutoring. It sounded like fun, so I inquired. However, there was an entrance exam. The next step was getting permission from my mom. After I spoke with her, she agreed. I took the test and passed.

"In the back of my mind, passing this test was a bad thing, and I requested to retake it. Big mistake! But, my wishes were granted; I retook the test and failed on purpose. Unbeknownst to me, failing meant remedial classes. Bad idea! The mistake stayed with me for the duration of high school. I did not fail another grade."

"OMG! You had to be in remedial classes throughout high school? Couldn't you take a test to get out of there, like you did to get in?" Aniyah asked.

"I wish. My ignorance did not stop with this incident. The same guys I skipped class with were the kids I got suspended with again. We decided it would be fun to kick the chalkboard in the next classroom so the teacher could not teach. What was I thinking? Yes, we got away and no one saw us, except I left my shoe impression on the board. Lucky me!"

Aniyah shook her head at Julian's actions, but he was only a sixth grader seeking attention of belonging or being accepted by someone. He learned that trying to fit with the in-crowd cost him a lot of humanity.

"So, time moved on and pretty soon I was in eighth grade. Graduation was coming, and I wanted a nice suit. My choice was to get a job. The only place I could find was Subway, but since I was underage, they paid me under the table. It forced me to learn responsibility.

"Luckily, my mother decided I had made many improvements and agreed to help me get my license. But that did not last long. I crashed my mother's car into the neighbor's wrought-iron fence. I had to come up with 600 dollars to fix their fence. My driving privileges ended before they even started.

"The thrill of driving and my ignorance kicked in; I figured out where my aunt kept her car keys. My friends and I drove to school events and took joyrides through town. It lasted for a few months. Then one day, a neighbor saw us and told my aunt. Our days of stealing the car ended immediately.

"Since I couldn't drive anymore and keeping my job was important, the only option left was to ride the bus. I was learning work ethics. One night coming home from work, I decided it would be more fun to jump the turnstile instead of paying. I had the money in my pocket, and the police found it. I was arrested, and my mother had to come bail me out. Needless to say, my next several paychecks went towards paying her back. The old saying, 'If your friend jumped off a cliff, would you?' rang true to me at that time."

"Julian, whatever possessed you to do such a stupid thing?"

"Good question. I have no idea. I guess it was about being cool in front of my friends."

"Your friends were with you?" she replied.

"No… but I could have told them about it the next day. I continued to struggle with school, home life and friends. My choices gradually got worse until my family thought I took a turn to the streets. I was slowly becoming an entrepreneur. The kid down the street wanted a bike. Since the job kept up my cash flow, I sold him my bike and bought a new one. I made a few bucks and had a brand-new bike. However, he decided not to pay me the money he owed. A businessman cannot make a living if his clients don't pay, so I went to collect. When he refused, I threatened him. It was my second offense as a juvenile.

"The curfew violation and this incident almost landed me in a correctional facility. Thank God my mother got a lawyer to represent me. At that point, I knew things had to stop, but stupidity kicked in many more times."

"So… that was not the end?" she wondered.

"Not even close."

"Okay, I said it was crazy to tell me all this stuff, but continue. Now, I want to hear what happened."

"Really?"

"Yep! Continue," she said with a smile. Julian liked to see her happy.

"I have learned that confidence comes with age, but it's the act of participating in different events that gives you the knowledge. My self-assurance began to improve in high school. It was the first time in my life I was popular, not only with the basketball team but also with the ladies."

"The ladies?" she said sternly.

Julian nodded. "We can't always control every situation, but we can alter the way you handle the problem. You have a choice either to learn from the mistake and move forward or stay stuck in a situation that is killing you one small piece at a time. It was time to change my actions, and take responsibility for my behavior.

"The one thing that stuck with me throughout school was enduring the remedial classes. All the classrooms were on a specific side of the campus, so I would be tardy in order to keep the other kids from seeing me enter the classroom. But one morning, my plan failed when one of my friends saw me enter the classroom. The ridicule ensued. I'm sure it was well-deserved.

"The school kids knew me, from the freshmen to the seniors. My complexion cleared, which helped with my acceptance. Plus, being able to drive was a bonus. Although I did take driver's education, my issue with speed cost me my license. The rules did not apply at this point."

"Well, you have changed. I have never seen you speed."

"Yep! I have learned my lesson. Plus, maturity helped. I slipped past on the first speeding ticket; technically I could have gone to jail for doing fifty-six miles per hour over the speed limit. I pled guilty, paid a fine and did five days of SWAP (Sheriff's Work Alternative Program) for eight hours each day. In SWAP we cleaned up the city wearing orange vests, picking up trash and raking leaves. Sadly, this ticket was the first of many. Do you want me to stop? It's getting late," he asked.

"No… please go on. It's time to move past this mess."

"I am so glad you agree. My dream finally came true: I made the basketball team, and we became city champs that year. But, I was only able to play three of my four years because the coach implied that he felt threatened by my presence. He also said I wasn't going to be anything, but a thug.

"That moment changed my life. A deep-seated drive forced me to become a more successful man than the coach. As a child, those words meant everything, especially coming from my coach. Maybe he was right; I was stigmatized because of my involvement with my cousins.

"In many ways, the message was spot on. People thought I sold drugs because of my cousin. So, the term birds of a feather flock together is so true. Then, the inevitable happened. A police officer pulled me over while driving to school. He searched my car for three hours looking for drugs. The thing that scared me the most was his knowledge of my name, school, where I lived and who my friends were. He went on to say that he knew exactly what would become of me in the future. I knew the police were watching my every move. I was never involved in anything illegal, but no one wanted to believe in me, especially my family."

"I am glad you stayed out of that situation," Aniyah replied.

"No kidding, right? During my sophomore year, I was robbed at gunpoint; my money, jewelry, and wallet were stolen. It was the worst thing I have ever experienced. Someone holding a gun to your chest and taking everything you own. The robber's words ring clear today: 'If you make another move, I will kill you.'"

"OMG… Julian. I can't imagine what you must have gone through."

"Yes, but it did not stop there. I was robbed again in my senior year leaving a football game. A male with four friends approached and demanded I give up my coat. My response, 'NO!'

"He smacked me in the back with an aluminum bat and I took off running. He didn't have the opportunity to take my coat. The next day, I came back with my friends to look for the robbers and teach them a lesson. I didn't want to buy a gun, so the next best thing was a bat."

"Wait… I'm glad you decided not to buy a gun, Julian. It could have taken you down a bad road."

"I did… As I look back on the incident, I believe it was a set-up to get my stuff. The kids were jealous. I was one of the few who had their second car, dressed nice and had a job. The extent people go to to steal from someone else is amazing."

"Well, keep going. This is better than TV," she said in jest.

"Okay, very funny. Well, I moved past the situation, but another one took its place. An altercation popped up between another classmate and me. The argument was relayed to his cousin, and the next day I was approached by a much older man.

"This time a shotgun was held to my chest. He said, 'If you mess with my cousin again, I got this for you.' I immediately froze. "I wanted to take care of the situation, but that cop's words rang loud and clear."

Aniyah took a deep breath. "So… you let it go?"

"Yes, although it wasn't easy. I am proud of myself for letting it go."

"By now I was in senior year, which rolled out a new adventure. I continued to work, got a girlfriend, finally kept my driver's license, and was popular. What else could a young man want? Right…

"The sad thing was, my future remained the farthest thought from my mind. College was not even a consideration, nor was my plan after I graduated. A GPA was a foreign concept to me; the only concern I had was passing all my classes. Re-doing twelfth grade was not an option. I was the first of three people in my family to graduate. I left school in the dark.

"I was seventeen, graduated, and had had over five jobs. But with no plan, things stagnated. Which meant in the back of my mind, it was time to shake things up. At one job I truly disliked, I got the bright idea to steal shoes. It was a salesman job at the mall. After that, I worked at a few banquet halls and a movie theatre. All before I turned eighteen."

"Wow!" It was all she could muster.

"Situations occur that impact your life in more ways than you could ever predict. In my case, it was the police officer explaining reality. My education and the possible future I faced, according to his assessment. The advice struck a nerve, so I graduated and found my passion."

"Julian, we have to stop for the night. I want to hear more, but let's continue tomorrow, okay?"

"Yes, I am tired. But, do you still love me after knowing the truth?"

"Really…?"

The two giggled, and Julian knew the truth will always set you free. A weight that he'd carried since childhood had been lifted. It was indeed a blessing.

Chapter Nine:

Expecting

Aniyah found herself starting to enjoy being pregnant. It gave her a closeness she'd never felt before. She'd spend the last hour of her shift with the circus. The fetus did somersaults, and was mastering the trampoline. As time passed, the baby became more active.

A storm was developing, so the temperature was cooler that day, and the sky was filled with clouds. It was a perfect day for a stroll on the beach. Aniyah needed to stretch her legs and get some exercise. The walking helped the fluid retention in her legs, although it didn't do much for her aching back. Julian was making sure she didn't avoid her exercises.

Down the street from the coffee shop was a thrift store, except most of the clothes looked brand new; she bought a swimsuit and cover up. After changing at work, she headed for the beach. Her emotions raced between joy over the pregnancy and the fear of possibility of losing her husband. One minute she giggled about the baby kicking her in the ribs, and the next she was crying over Julian. It was difficult to stay on track from one second to the next, but today Aniyah was looking forward to some time alone at the beach. One of her co-workers showed her a section of the beach, away from tourists. They had become residents of Hawaii, one place she never imagined living.

Aniyah grabbed her make-shift picnic basket and beach essentials. She borrowed an umbrella from her boss and headed for the ocean. The sand tickled between her toes, it felt good to walk barefoot. She glanced out at the horizon, watching the seagulls soaring on the wind currents.

"Ahhh," she thought. The warm breeze felt good, cooling the perspiration on her body.

She trekked up the coastline to a curve in the beach. The water sloshed against the rocks as the waves rolled along the strand. It was an incredible sight. It wasn't home, but Aniyah had become fond of their temporary home. She pulled out the beach blanket and lunch basket, put up under her umbrella, and it was time to rest her weary back. The plan to relax worked.

Aniyah leaned back in her chair and closed her eyes. The waves continued to rock her into serenity. It was the first time all day the baby was quiet, an event that was easy to notice these days. But the doctor told them an active fetus is a healthy one, something to be grateful under the circumstances. The concept of becoming a parent and developing the unconditional love for someone you've never seen was miraculous. No one could ever understand until they become a parent, but only a mother can truly comprehend the closeness. It's an unbreakable bond, one Aniyah would cherish forever.

Several hours had passed and it was time to pack up her things and head for the hospital. Julian would be getting worried. It was so easy to pretend their predicament didn't exist while relaxing on the beach. "Well, baby, we have to go see you daddy," Aniyah stated.

The drive to see Julian was a sober one; his condition worsened each day. Most times, he was only awake for a few hours a day. He tried to rest during the daylight hours so they had more time together in the evenings.

"Hi baby, how are you today?" Aniyah asked.

"I'm good, come here and give me a kiss." She smiled; his pretense of cheer was appreciated.

Julian knew the pressure his wife was under. It gave him the will to keep fighting. "How's my little baby today?"

"Oh, you have no idea. All afternoon I got one kick to the ribs after another."

"Can I feel?" Julian gleamed with excitement.

"Sure, next time I'll tell you."

"Perfect! I missed you last night, but it's alright. You need some space and time to yourself."

"I know, I missed you as well. My sister says to send her love. We talked, and then I took a bath and went to sleep."

"What else happened today?"

"Not much, work went well, and I went to the beach."

"Oh, I hate being stuck in here."

"I know… but what about your past, where we left off the other night? Do you want to talk some more?"

"Maybe just a few more things. Are you alright with that?"

"Yes, go ahead," she replied.

"I learned over the years that life is meant to have hurdles, but most people think of them as failures and give up on their dreams. In actuality, these speed bumps are meant to teach us lessons. If you can turn a negative into a positive, the glass is always half full. No matter the situation, you can prevail with flying colors. We must think of life as a series of lessons, each one bringing us closer to the goals we set for ourselves."

"I'm still working on the lesson to be learned in this case," she stated sincerely.

"I know…" Julian swallowed hard, and then continued:

"My goal to be in law enforcement manifested itself due to my determination. I hadn't made my way to being a police officer yet, but I was one step closer to making my dreams come true. My new job allowed me to concentrate on graduating from college, although I was surprised when my professor failed me in English. In my mind, I was young and charismatic, so wooing her was easier. But she didn't fall for my expectations. The difficulties I experienced in high school left my writing skills sub-par. Now, in the past I would have gotten mad and walked away or blamed someone else for my problems. Maturity has a way of changing your personality. The professor forced me to accept responsibility. I became a better writer and realized if you want something worth having, it requires work. I am thankful for her tutoring.

"Although I faced numerous road blocks, it never stopped me from putting my best foot forward. I graduated with my undergraduate degree in criminal justice. Plus, I made it through the academy. It took me three tries to pass, but I knew at this point God had something special planned for my life.

"The degree satisfied me for the moment and I decided to focus on becoming the best officer in the facility. So, I went to the library and found as many books as I could on law to study whenever I had free time. My accomplishments increased my self-esteem substantially.

"I was twenty-three with a bachelor's degree and my own place. I worked two jobs; one would think I was successful. But, you can't judge a book by its cover. My monthly living expenses were overwhelming. I had to pawn valuable items and take out car title loans to cover the bills. Lesson learned: things can always get worse.

"The outward appearance of my success gave me an attitude of invincibility. My intoxicated revelry on the weekends saw me arrive home several times alive, but with no memory of driving. After one Saturday night of partying, I hit a guardrail on the expressway and nearly totaled my car. My injuries were serious, but luckily not life threatening."

"Oh my God, Julian. You could have been killed," Aniyah stated.

"I know… It was a wake-up call. I skated past the accident without legal troubles and did not lose my job."

"You were lucky."

"Yes, I was. During the next month when a prisoner escaped, I got my first major break. The police report read about a man who assaulted a police officer and stole his gun, then ran. He was high, holding a stolen gun, and loaded with ecstasy pills. I can only imagine how difficult that arrest was to make. The guy was out of his mind on drugs for weeks. It made the situation very dangerous.

"We got the call while on patrol. When I finally caught him and struggled to get him handcuffed, one thing became clear: I was tall, skinny, with no stamina and weak."

"I can't imagine," she giggled. Julian laughed.

"The very next morning, I began a workout regimen. Since I was embarrassed to be seen in public, the workouts started at home, and then moved to the gym after I gained some confidence."

"That's more like the Julian I know!"

"A few months later, an offer to join the DEA (Drug Enforcement Administration) came through. But being stubborn, I declined due to another academy option. I regret that choice.

"My past haunted me; it's what kept me all over the map. Over the next twelve months, I took the fireman and state trooper exam. I'd jump into these wild decisions, not knowing why I kept making them. Maybe it's because I was making $8.50 an hour as part-time police officer? The jobs veered from my end goal. It all boiled down to patience. But, the one goal I maintained was being a highly decorated officer within my department, despite the pay. It allowed me to work in several departments over the first year.

"My performance offered many honorable mentions and officer of the month awards. Although, I was still making $8.50 an hour and working two jobs to make ends meet."

"Oh… Julian that is not much."

"No, not when you have bills to pay. I had to keep searching for part-time opportunities. I was learning to stay the course. But when I thought things were lining up and running smooth, another obstacle showed itself.

"My performance granted me the opportunity to work with trainees. 'Great,' I thought. A guy was brought in for selling drugs on the street. After he was processed and his belongings were logged, I gave my student the chance to learn how the chain of custody worked. The next day when I came in for my shift, the sergeant wanted to see me in his office. He passed along the news that my trainee stole the money from the inventory bag on the way downstairs. As the senior officer, all incidents, good or bad, were my responsibility.

"The investigation put me on suspension without pay. I had to surrender my badge and go home. Needless to say, the situation left me devastated. How could I have made such a careless mistake?"

"Wow! Did you catch him?"

"Yes, a few hours later the trainee returned the money and apologized for the stress he caused myself and the department. He explained that the money was for his family. I was so excited to get my badge back. Soon after the situation, I found another opportunity to become part-time. The hours were better with improved pay."

"Thank God."

"I know, right? Well, the new department allowed me to work with men who could teach me to be a great officer. I received many awards from the department in three months. On my way home from work one night I happened to hear the radio transmission given from dispatch about a home invasion. Dispatch stated, '3-4 masked men with guns tied-up the homeowners and their children with ropes, and they are taking everything they own.' Without hesitation I sprang into action. After a 40-minute pursuit, all the suspects, their guns, and the victims' belongings were recovered. The victims were unharmed. They called me their hero! God's plan revealed itself."

"Oh! Julian, put your hand right here." Julian's face lit up.

"Really?" Aniyah sat and watched her husband gleam with pride over feeling his baby move the first time.

"Thank you, God," she whispered.

Julian laid his hands on her stomach and just enjoyed the moment. It was great to be alive.

Chapter Ten:

The Recurring Event

Aniyah sat in the parking lot contemplating her next course of action. She wanted to find some support without having to explain the whole situation again. It seemed it had become a reoccurring event as of late. The idea struck her to take a walk on the beach after work. The ocean was something she'd never been around much and it was alluring. Its soothing sound could calm anyone's fears.

A hot bubble bath was just the ticket. Besides, she had promised to call her sister. It been about a week since they talked and she needed to hear a friendly voice. Someone that intimately understood their situation.

It was only a short walk to her new apartment and she did not have to deal with rush hour traffic. Aniyah had to admit the one great thing about being in Hawaii was the mild driving conditions. They'd been gone for almost seven months and she didn't miss rush hour traffic driving home from work every night. She'd grown accustomed to the weather; the heat was more difficult. Plus, seeing the sun every day was kind of weird.

"Ahh, home sweet home," Aniyah thought to herself. "A hot bath, just what the doctor ordered." Although, she hated that Julian was stuck in that hospital bed relentlessly. He was never lazy, and part of his routine was exercise. As a matter of fact, it had been several months since he'd been outside. It was hard to fathom.

"Hey, sis, how are you?" Aniyah asked.

"I'm good, but more importantly, how are you?"

"I feel pregnant! I'm good, but it's getting harder to move around each day."

"I can imagine. How is Julian? What did he say about the baby? Does he know what you're having?"

"Oh, he is so excited. I did not tell him, wanted it to be a surprise. But, sis he gets weaker every day. I'm worried. What if…"

"Stop, don't even think that way," Sofia replied.

"I'm trying not to, but it's hard here being alone. I was just walking around today, thinking about how much I miss you guys."

"We miss you, chica," Sofia told her sister.

"So, if I have this baby in Hawaii, are you going to fly here to be with me? It won't be long now."

"You know we will be on the first plane. Mom, Dad and I were talking about that last night."

"Ohhh, thank you. I feel much better."

"Well, sis, I have to run. Talk next week, right? Or sooner if you need me?"

"Yes, I will call if something happens. I love you," Aniyah replied.

"I love you more. Talk soon."

It was hard hanging up with her family. She felt so alone without them nearby. But, either way, it was almost over. A hot soak calmed Aniyah's fears for the short term.

Chapter Eleven:

In the Moment

Aniyah loved the soothing touch of her husband. His soft warm hands felt good as he waited with anticipation for the baby to move one more time. The hospital room became a normal part of life over the last seven months. But, she worried their time together was coming to an end. Constant recommendations told them don't be negative, although that was easier said than done.

It was thrilling to watch Julian envelop himself in the moment. The baby was one of the few things he had to cherish, being stuck in this hospital. "Julian… I need to lie down. It's been a long day."

"Of course, come on over here," he stated excitedly.

The beat of his heart calmed all her apprehensions. She snuggled in tight and he wrapped his arm around her side, resting his palm on her stomach. "I love you," she told him.

"I love you too, babe. See ya in the morning."

"Absolutely. Plus, I want to hear the rest of your story."

"Alright, sounds good."

Aniyah drifted off thinking about her daughter. "What will she look like," she thought. She couldn't wait to touch her soft delicate skin, see her laugh for the first time, even change diapers. It was the one shining element of the future she could look forward to. They'd have many talks about her daddy over the years to come. It was imperative she learned of his honest compassion for others, and especially, his love for life.

Over the last many months, Aniyah had time to accept her destiny. She knew raising her daughter alone would be challenging, but it was a hurdle she'd overcome no matter what happened. All she could do was pray for a miracle and plan for the worst.

It was crazy to think how the sounds of a hospital room could be soothing, but the humming of the machines and pulsing of the oxygen tanks lulled her to sleep every night.

Julian lay awake, watching his bride sleep in a restful slumber. He couldn't imagine life without her being by his side. It was terrifying to think about dying and leaving them alone. Faith told him that God would protect them; nonetheless he wanted to be their knight. He thought about all the things he wanted to do with his son; play baseball, watch him graduate college, and most of all, see the refrigerator filled with drawings saying "Daddy, I love you!"

The thought brought tears to his eyes when he imagined not seeing a future with his family. Life had been reduced to a hospital room. His gratitude remained strong, but he fought back the anger. It was difficult to keep his feelings to himself, but Aniyah must never know about the frustration he felt. She had enough on her plate to deal with at the moment.

Aniyah knew deep down how Julian was feeling; they'd been together for a long time, and it was pointless trying to keep anything quiet. She read him like a book, although Aniyah appreciated his concern for her well-being. It was time for him to just be honest and tell the truth.

"Julian can you move your arm so I can get up?" she whispered. Her response went unnoticed. "Julian... I have to use the bathroom." Aniyah felt a sickening feeling in her stomach, drawing her full attention. She pushed his arm away from her neck and sat up.

"Julian… please wake up." Duress took over. Aniyah was shaking. "Nurse!" she screamed. "Someone help, please!"

Aniyah climbed out of bed and ran to the door, "Nurse, someone please help me!" The hallway was quiet and the nurse's station was empty. *What's going on, where is everyone?* she wondered. As she walked around the central desk, a pain doubled her over. "Ohhh…" she gasped. "What the he-" slipped out.

When the pain subsided, she headed back to their room, but not before another contraction surged through her body. Aniyah grabbed the wall for support. "HELP!" she screamed. Her calls for assistance fell on deaf ears. As she worked her way back to Julian, a sound echoed off the walls into the hallway. "It can't be! nooooooo," she pleaded. The bone chilling flatline. It was impossible for her to move any faster with the contractions crippling her movement.

"Aniyah, wake up!" someone whispered.

"What! Oh my God, my baby is coming!" she shouted.

"No, honey, you're dreaming. Come on, I'll help you get up. We have to move you out of the way."

The words hit hard. "What's wrong? Julian..." she sobbed.

"Come on, let me help you," the nurse repeated.

Aniyah sat on the edge of the chair, doubled over at the idea of her husband really dying. *God please bring him back*, she repeated in her head. The sounds of the staff vanished as she sat praying to wake up from this horrible nightmare.

"Ahhhhhh!" she screeched.

"Aniyah....?" The nurse called out. "Are you alright?"

"No... I'm really going into labor."

"What, now? You sure?" the nurse asked.

"Yes, now!" Everyone in the room stopped.

"Alright, come on. I'll call your doctor." Aniyah fell to her knees; she couldn't walk any longer. "Orderly, get me a wheelchair!" the nurse shouted. "I've gotcha Aniyah, hold on."

In the distance, Aniyah heard a change in tone, "Do you hear that?" she asked. "Is Julian…"

"Maybe… I'll go check when I get you settled, alright?" Aniyah nodded. It was no use hiding her tears at this point. The nurse held her hand. There were no words to relieve the agony.

The orderly arrived with the wheelchair. "Please… check for me, please?" she begged.

"Take her down to the delivery room, and I'll meet you there," the nurse said.

"Yes, ma'am," he replied. "Hi, Aniyah. I'm Grady. I am so sorry for your loss."

"LOSS?! What do you mean?" she shouted.

"Oh… no, I just thought…" he replied.

"Sorry, I did not mean to yell at you. It's just…"

"You don't have to explain. I understand," said Grady.

"Do you know something about my husband, Grady?"

"No... I just saw you crying and thought he was..."

"Okay, that is a relief. I think," she replied.

Aniyah tried to keep her mind focused on the baby and her delivery. It was better than the alternative. "Aniyah I will leave you right here, and get a nurse," Grady stated.

"Yes, I'm fine. Go ahead," she told him. The contractions subsided somewhat.

"Maybe it was false labor?" she wondered.

"Aniyah, I am Nurse Webber. Are you doing alright?" She nodded. "We are preparing you a room right now. Will your husband be joining you?"

The question brought uncontrollable sobbing once again. "No-" she shook her head.

"I'm so sorry. I did not mean to upset you," the nurse replied.

"It's okay, you did not know," she struggled to speak. "He is upstairs in the long-term care ward. Julian is on the heart transplant list. I just left him, he was coding when I went into labor. I-"

"Oh, my gosh."

"The nurse was supposed to come down and give me an update," she stated.

"I will send someone to find out. We can't have you down here in labor wondering what happened."

"Thank you," she replied. Aniyah sat against the wall by the nurse's station, practicing her Lamaze breathing. It was the only thing that kept her from passing out. The nurses came back after about fifteen minutes and pushed her to a delivery room.

"Here we go, Aniyah. Let me get you in bed and I will check on your husband's status. The doctor will be here soon to check on your status."

"Okay," she mustered.

"Here, I brought you a box of tissues and some water." Aniyah didn't really care about anything except Julian. The pressure made her feel like she was about to explode.

"How long does it take to get an update?" Aniyah wondered. "Breathe, you must breathe."

Chapter Twelve:

It's Almost Time

"Aniyah, we're almost there. One more push. I can see the head."

"Ohhhh," she retorted.

"That's it. I have her, you can relax," the doctor stated. Aniyah took a sign of relief. "Aniyah… don't panic, but we have to rush you into surgery. You have a tear in the lining of the uterus, and we need to fix that. We put the anesthesia in your IV so you'll be getting sleepy very quickly. You can see you daughter for a few minutes, but then we have to get this fixed."

Aniyah was too tired and sleepy to react, so she just shrugged at the statement and took her baby for a few minutes. "Oh, baby… how are you? I am your mommy. I love you, see you very soon," she told her daughter.

The medication had taken hold and Aniyah fell into a deep sleep. "Alright, nurse get her into surgery. We'll have this fixed in a jiffy. Oh, any word on her husband?"

"I was going to check the status, but I know she has family in the waiting room," the nurse told the doctor.

"Good... I will go update them on Aniyah and the infant."

The doctor proceeded to the waiting room to inform the family of Aniyah's status. "Hello, I am Dr. Waters. We had to take Aniyah into surgery. She had a small tear in the lining of her uterus and it had to be fixed. Otherwise she and baby are doing fantastic. She had a baby girl, and should be in the nursery shortly. The nurse was cleaning her up when I left. I will come back and give you an update when Aniyah is in recovery. Oh... yes, do you know what's happening with her husband Julian?"

"The only thing they told us is his situation is critical and it would not be much longer. They were trying to get him stable so he could at least see his daughter."

The doctor looked worried since no one had an update on Julian. "Thank you. Let me see if I can find out something for you, alright?"

"Thanks doc," Sofia stated. He nodded and left the waiting room.

Shortly after the doctor left, she heard the nurses talking about some emergency helicopter landing and for everyone to be ready to accept the package.

Sofia wondered, "Could it be a heart for Julian?"

It was difficult to just sit and wait; she hated being there alone. But the rest of her family would not be arriving until late evening. Their plane was held up due to bad weather.

Sofia sat in the waiting room thinking about how excited Aniyah was when she called about being pregnant. It was something she and Julian had wanted for quite some time. The hours passed, people came and went, TV shows started and stopped. But, just as Sofia thought the wait would never end, the nurse came in and said she could come see her niece.

Sofia ran into the doctor on the way, "Sofia, Aniyah will be fine, she is in recovery. You can see her shortly."

"Oh... thank you. Praise the Lord! Any word on Julian?"

"No, I am afraid not," he replied.

"Let me take you to see the baby and I will call down to the ICU and see what they say, alright?"

"God bless you, thanks," she stated sincerely.

Sofia stood in front of the nursery looking for her niece, when the attendant smiled. "I'll get her," she motioned.

It was unimaginable how people can fall in love with a baby at first sight. Sofia couldn't take her eyes off the infant. Aniyah would be so happy to see her daughter.

Then a nurse walked around the corner. "Are you Mrs. Parker's sister?"

"Yes, I am. Can I see her now?"

"Yes, she is asking for you."

"Great, thank you."

"Just follow me," the nurse stated.

Aniyah was awake and smiling when Sofia entered the recovery room. It caught her off guard. "Hi, sis. How are you feeling?" She was hesitant to ask.

"I am great! Did you see my baby?"

"Yes, she is beautiful! I must admit, you are much happier than I expected."

"Why, should I not be?"

Sofia looked puzzled, not knowing how to react.

"You haven't heard, have you?" Aniyah asked.

"No, what?"

"Julian is going to be okay. They took him into surgery about an hour ago. The doctor said he is expecting good results. Oh... my God! I am so happy! But they said it's about a six-hour surgery."

"Really? Wow," Sofia replied.

"Sofia, can you come with me, we are going to get Aniyah moved back up to her room. It will take about an hour, and you can meet us up there, okay?" The nurse asked.

"Yes, what room number?"

"455 on the maternity floor."

"Perfect, I'll be in the nursery. Hey, can I hold the baby?"

"Yes, if Aniyah signs a waiver."

Aniyah spoke up, "Bring it over. She can hold the baby!"

Sofia agreed to the terms, and after they were signed, she headed back to the nursery. Spending time with her niece was the best gift ever. Aniyah waited impatiently for some news; the reality of Julian's heart transplant hadn't sunk in yet. She had accepted the idea of raising her daughter alone, so the information was surreal. They faced a long road with his recovery, but a miracle had been granted.

"Hi, Aniyah how are you feeling?" the nurse asked. "My name is Amanda. If you are feeling better, I will bring the baby in for you. Well, after I chase down your sister," she giggled.

Aniyah laughed, "Yes, she loves babies. You might have to put on your running shoes." The nurse smiled.

It was an exciting moment she had waited nine months to witness. A few minutes later, her sister came walking in with her daughter. "Olivia... this is your mommy," Sofia stated.

Aniyah's eyes filled with tears, "Come here to Mommy, Olivia. You are so beautiful."

Sofia gleamed with pride; it was wonderful to see her sister smile again. The last ten months had been a nightmare for everyone.

"Sofia... I am so glad you are here with me," Aniyah stated.

"Me too," she replied.

"I hope we get some word on Julian soon," Aniyah commented.

"I know, honey. It should not be much longer. He said six hours, and that will be in about thirty minutes."

"Okay, thank goodness." The baby yawed, and Aniyah felt the exhaustion setting in fast. "Sofia, do you mind if we take a short nap? I want to be awake when Julian comes out of surgery."

"Sure, I will go downstairs and get some dinner. See you soon. Besides, Mom and Dad should be here soon as well," she replied.

"Great! I can't wait to see them. I love you!"

"I love you too!" Sofia left the room so Mommy and baby could rest. It was a glorious day for their family.

Aniyah's parents arrived shortly after Sofia came back from the cafeteria. They were in the waiting room when Dr. McCarthy came in with an update on Julian. "I have news on Julian," he stated.

"Wait… can we go into Aniyah's room with the baby so she can hear it with us?'

"Sure, what room?"

"Follow me, I'll take you," Sofia stated.

Aniyah was awake and getting ready to feed the baby for the first time as they entered. The nurse greeted them at the door, "Oh, doctor, can we have a few minutes?"

"I came to update everyone on Julian," he replied.

"Let them in!" Aniyah shouted. The nurse stepped back and her family entered behind the doctor.

"Julian… is he alright?"

"Yes, he will be in recovery most of the night. But, all went well and there's no sign of rejection at this point, which is fantastic. We will watch him closely over the next 24 hours to be sure. Congratulations on your baby. She is beautiful," Dr. McCarthy stated.

"Oh… that is the best news I've ever heard. The family that donated the heart, can we send them a thank you for their sacrifice?" Aniyah asked.

"Yes, I will have someone from the donation department come and speak with you. But, for now all looks good. Get some rest, and I'll check in with you in the morning." The family nodded.

"My God! I am so relieved to know Julian will be alright. He is going to live. It's been a nightmare over the last ten months living with this mess, not knowing from one minute to the next if he would even survive long enough to get a heart. As it turns out he almost did not; the doctors had given him several hours."

"Aniyah, we are so happy for you both. Now, can I see my granddaughter?"

"Sure," she smiled. *It's good to have family around again*, she thought.

They laughed and talked most of the night. Considering the situation, the nurses granted special privileges for the family to stay after visiting hours.

Julian woke about 4 a.m. "Can I get some water?" he called on his intercom. The nurses rushed in, grateful to see him up and alert.

"Is my wife coming back soon? Can we call her?" he asked.

"Sure, but you won't need to call. She is upstairs in the maternity ward."

"What?!" he shouted.

"It's alright, everything is fine. You have a baby girl!" Julian was completely speechless.

The nurse smiled, "They have been waiting for you to wake up. Be right back," she replied.

Julian had no idea what to think: he was a father. The thought made his heart transplant seem minimal. His mind ran wild with thoughts about life. It's something we take for granted at times, and don't give our mortality enough consideration. We just run from day to day, caught up in the rigmarole of society and forget to give thanks. It's only when a catastrophe takes place do we stop and ponder the priceless veracity of our existence.

The voices in the corridor startled Julian, who was lost in his meditation. Aniyah walked in first holding the baby. "Olivia…" was all he could muster.

The tears rolled down Julian's cheeks as he took his daughter in his arms and fell in love immediately. Aniyah watched in awe at the sight before her eyes. They were truly blessed with a miracle.

"Aniyah, she is beautiful, just like her mother. I love you!"

"I love you… Julian Parker."

Chapters Thirteen:

In the Blink of an Eye

Julian woke up early on the last Tuesday morning he had to spend in the hospital. After a year in the ICU and three months of rehabilitation, it was finally time to go home. Julian longed to go back to work. It was as though he'd been given a new start on life, a second chance to make things right.

Since Olivia was born, Aniyah stayed in the apartment at night. It was the only way for the baby to sleep in peace. Julian learned very quickly how one little human could alter your perception of the future. In the blink of an eye, Olivia became the center of his world forever.

Julian learned life is filled with hurdles, and sometimes those obstacles become brick walls. But, in actuality, these speed bumps are meant to teach lessons. Being able to turn a negative into a positive situation reveals an understanding that no situation is insurmountable.

One lesson Julian learned without a doubt was remaining vigilant about your passions. Even being faced with death, he never truly lost faith. Somehow, he knew his mortality would be delayed. The memories of his youth captivated his every thought over the last few weeks. It was as though a burning desire to reflect on what happened came over his soul.

Julian went from struggling as a young child to a determined man fighting to pursue his dream job. His constant battle to overcome difficulties never faltered. His goal to become a law enforcement officer manifested itself due to pure fortitude. However, the charismatic college student learned that wooing his teacher failed at every attempt, which left him with a failed grade in English. The difficulties he faced in high school left Julian's writing skills sub-par. In the past, he found himself walking away from challenges only to blame someone else for his problems. But, his English professor forced him to accept responsibility. The end result proved to be worthwhile. Julian became an accomplished writer who understood the importance of hard work.

At times, Julian faced numerous roadblocks, but he always managed to put his best foot forward. He graduated with his undergraduate degree in criminal justice, plus the added bonus of graduating from the correctional academy after several attempts. Julian acknowledged the fact that God had something special planned for his life.

His inner stirrings were finally calmed, and he was able to focus on becoming the best law enforcement officer possible. It took hours of studying law books at the library, but the accomplishment built up his self-esteem substantially.

By that time, Julian was twenty-three with a college degree but found himself in debt. He was successful, nevertheless; you can't judge a book by its cover. Lesson learned: things can always get worse. He was forced to pawn valuable items to cover his monthly bills. Even working three jobs, he was unable to become financially independent. Julian's camouflage of success gave him an attitude of invincibility.

Over the next few months, things leveled off and life started to make sense. Behaviors became clear and Julian wanted to move forward without his past haunting him day and night.

Julian spent years trying to find his purpose, with one door closed in his face after another. The obstacles never seemed to stop. He endured his new position, but the salary issue was far from resolved. Julian went from $8.50 an hour to $13.50 and struggled to keep a roof over his head. Finally, after the home invasion arrest, the department offered him another raise, one that would take him out of debt. Things were coming together.

The moonlighting employment came to a halt after his next pay period. He quit his security jobs and started to work part-time with a youth organization. His choice proved valuable. Julian was given the job of juvenile officer, one more step in the right direction. Julian felt at ease with the decision; it was a God-designed purpose.

Julian's professional career moved in the right direction for the most part, but behind closed doors, he was still a mess. His outlet for the damage of the past was women. Almost every night, Julian hunted the town searching for Mrs. Right. It was an empty void that could not be filled; bar hopping to find a soulmate never works.

Once Julian's finances started to level off and he was freed from his debt, he moved into a new apartment. One he was proud to entertain his guests in. Finally, Julian met the woman of his dreams. She was smart, funny, and beautiful. The money flowed freely, and they had a great time. He loved his career and the nights with his new love, Nicole. Life was grand!

One morning, Julian left early for work and Nicole was still sleeping. Another officer called in sick and he took his place. A quick note left on the counter explained why he had to leave so early.

Due to his money issues, he chose to work a double shift, which gave him an hour break to eat and change clothes. The eagerness to have someone at home waiting for him was exhilarating.

When he returned on his hour break to change clothes, the sight at home left him altered. Nicole was sitting on the edge of the couch in a tattered state. Her response was unexpected; apparently, his absence was inexcusable. This had led to her trashing the house, breaking pictures, spray painting walls and destroying the kitchen. The severed relationship forced Julian to move once again, but he accepted the situation and started seeing other women. However, over the next several months, he dealt with constant damage to his car.

Julian continued to file police reports on every incident, but with no leads, the issue continued to escalate. Then, the situation evolved into threatening letters: "I found you and you hurt me; now I'm going to hurt you like you hurt me!"

The message caught Julian off guard; his escapades with these women had to stop immediately. His situation escalated to broken car windows and flowers being delivered to the station with accusatory notes. At one point, he was almost put on suspension. The department gave him a certain amount of time to get the situation under control, and this warning clarified the seriousness of the situation.

Instead of dealing with the situation, Julian continued to seek out women. Many were only one-night stands. A close friend pulled him aside and sternly scolded him for not taking the incidents seriously, and the point was taken to heart. Julian spent the night thinking about his recent decisions.

The next day after his shift, instead of bar hopping he started looking at video footage of businesses near the apartment to see if he recognized any of the women. A few weeks later, his car was egged and thankfully it was caught on video. The suspect was arrested. It was time to change direction immediately. Julian moved once again to a new area of town and bought another cell phone. He left his old number and life in the past.

Julian was startled out of his reminiscence when the discharge nurse entered his room. "Julian…" she called.

He turned to look. "Hi! I'm sorry, I was lost in thought."

"It's okay. How are you feeling?" she asked.

"I am great! I have not stepped outside in six months. Don't take this personal, but I hope to never set foot in another hospital again. At least, not for a long time." He smiled.

"Oh, I completely understand," she replied. "I will have you discharged within the hour."

Julian breathed a deep sigh of relief. It was finally real; they were going home.

Chapters Fourteen:

Little Angel

Julian waited eagerly for Aniyah and his baby girl to arrive. It was almost unbearable. He had been waiting for this meeting for too long.

The nurse giggled about his anxious state of mind. "Julian you're like a kid at Christmas. Since I have known you, I've not seen you so excited about anything. It's adorable."

Julian smiled. "I've been waiting for this day since I got the news about my heart. Only, at that time, I was not expecting to have a child right away."

"They change your whole world in a matter of seconds, don't they?"

"I had no idea. She is a miracle."

"Yes, and she will always be your baby, no matter how old she gets."

Julian giggled. "I have already imagined her at 14 when she tells me, 'Dad, I am not a child!'" The nurse laughed. She had been through the process with her own children.

"Well, my kids are grown and have their own babies. They now understand what I meant. I find it funny. It tickles me for them to call and say, Mom, how did you ever deal with us?"

Julian felt the embrace of heaven to be alive and blessed with a daughter. God always has a plan; we may not understand the reason things happen, but it's for the best.

In the midst of his daydreaming, he heard Aniyah and Olivia coming down the hall. It was easy to know when they entered the ward: The nurses went gaga over the baby. Only today, Julian was able to meet them at the door and greet his bride.

"Good morning, my love. Can I take her?" Aniyah smiled.

"Hello, Olivia. How are you today?" he asked the baby. She wiggled from the attention.

"Are you ready, Julian?" Aniyah asked.

"More than ready. I thought you'd never get here."

"I can only imagine. Well, I brought everything we need for a great day at the beach. Then, we head home in the morning," she smiled.

"I can't wait. Let's get out of here."

When Julian entered the hallway, he was greeted by a pleasant surprise. The nurses and doctor had planned a quick surprise party. A large cake sat on a cart in front of the nurse's station. "We will miss you, Julian. Have a wonderful life."

Julian stood completely dumbfounded. It was an unexpected treat! As the tears poured down his cheeks, joy filled his soul. He was truly blessed beyond belief. It had not occurred to him how fond of these people he had become over the last nine months. The incident he hated to think about had changed his life forever. Every staff member cared for him and Aniyah as if they were their own family. He would deeply miss their smiling faces.

"I don't know what to say, but thank you. If it was not for all of you, I would not be alive today. Your dedication to these people is incredible. I will always be grateful to every one of you. May the Lord bless all of your lives." The room cheered for Julian's heartfelt speech. "Now… let's have some cake. And everyone else in this ward who is able to share with us."

Aniyah looked at her husband, knowing their love had only blossomed during this time of suffering.

The group ate cake, laughed and enjoyed the pleasures of life before Julian departed the hospital for the last time. His heart ached to be outside in the fresh air and sunshine. Since their time in Hawaii, he'd only spent two days away from the hospital. They never even had a honeymoon. Although, today would be the best celebration of life anyone could ever imagine.

"Julian are you ready to go?" Aniyah asked.

"Yes, like, yesterday. I can't take it any longer." They said goodbye and headed for the beach.

Julian watched the bright sunlight glimmer off the glass doors as they exited the hospital. It was a sight to be cherished forever. His body ached to feel the warmth caress his skin.

The beach was a short walk from the hospital, so Julian insisted on making the trek on foot. Aniyah drove the car and met them at the coastline. It was as though all his senses were alive. Julian could hear the birds singing a cheerful cadence, the ocean breeze embracing his face with a touch of sea salt, but the most alluring was the sound of society. People walking the streets, eating at the local cafes, or surfers carrying their boards to the beach. It was an incredible sight, and Julian soaked up every nuance of the experience. With Olivia wrapped tight in his arms, he could not imagine a better scene to witness on the first day of his new life. He was taking every advantage possible with his second chance.

"Olivia… do you know how much Daddy loves you?" She just stared into his eyes. It was a gaze that would always take his breath away.

"I have to tell you something, Olivia. Once you make the conscious decision to start fresh and leave the past where it belongs, progress becomes a reality. You must learn to focus. If you spend too much time trying to make others happy, the only outcome will be disappointment. True friendship is a rare commodity, baby. The only way to have a stable relationship with anyone is to be comfortable with yourself. I want you to always remember those words. Your daddy has learned those lessons the hard way. My patience and blessings finally paid off, and I had an opportunity to work with the unit of my dreams. I have endured hardships and participated in things that made me feel shame, however I learned from the past and set my mind not to repeat old habits.

"I learned very quickly the best therapy is exercise. Whenever I came home frustrated or concerned, I worked-out and instantly my emotions calmed and clarity reigned. In seven years, I gained fifty pounds of muscle. The passion drove my career to a new level. I wanted to become a personal trainer. In my family health isn't a priority; however I started a new trend. The thought gave me motivation. During this last year, I realized how important exercise and healthy habits are to being happy and fulfilled. Now, I know you're just a baby and you probably won't remember anything I tell you today, but it's important that I tell you.

"My prayer was answered, and I was offered a position as a personal trainer. What a fantastic opportunity, it was thrilling, Olivia. But, things continued to progress when I received an email about an agility test for the department. The year before when I applied, they turned me down.

"I ran every day in preparation for the testing course. I finally achieved my objective: my dream job in the correctional department. When I notified the current department of my acceptance to the position, they offered me a promotion. The whole incident left me irritated, since I had been denied for a long time.

"My part-time job at the school was the one job I truly missed. Being able to help young kids find the right path and keep them on the straight and narrow was appealing. But, my prayers were coming to fruition. Olivia, my heart is with helping kids grow to successful adults." The baby snuggled in tight, completely content with her daddy.

"Then, Olivia, one afternoon at the gym, God blessed me beyond belief. I met your mama. The most beautiful woman I'd ever seen. Her presence made me weak; I loved every minute with her.

"I finally graduated from the academy, but money was tight. We struggled to make ends meet. Then out of eight hundred graduates, I was the only one missing a paycheck. Our rent was due and we only had a few dollars between us. My supervisor called human resources to rectify the situation, but he was informed of an incident that had happened ten years ago. They were unsure if I was supposed to have been hired, so this whole time nothing was said. By God's grace the storm faded, and I continued to pursue my dreams. My supervisor saw something in me, and I was asked to become the class leader. Class commander is an honored position. I almost cried, Olivia.

"I'd faced one obstacle after another, but I stayed true. Nothing could have prepared me for this moment. I said yes without a doubt.

"In a short period, I received several badges and continued with my education. The decision to take the class leader position separates the boys from the men, or the girls from the women in your case. I worked the graveyard shift and went to school during the day. In the afternoon, I had just enough time to take a short nap, and then repeat each day. Success comes at a price. You must be willing to make those concessions, Olivia. But don't worry, I'll be there every step of the way to teach you.

"In under two years I completed the graduate program. After graduation, it was time to focus on my personal training. I quit anything that didn't make me happy. Do you hear that, baby? If it doesn't bring you joy, leave it alone and move on.

"Your mom and I were in love. Our relationship progressed and we bought a house, the home you are going to grow up in, sweetheart. It was the first time in my life I owned anything of value that could bring us joy. We found a place to belong. When you maintain a relationship based on a strong foundation grounded in love and commitment you can achieve anything.

"I was finally making a decent living, but for years my colleagues got promotions and I was dismissed. It left me bitter for a long time. But I never gave up, and on the third attempt, I was granted the position."

"Hey, you two. I have been waiting for you," Aniyah called out.

"Oh… Hi, Mama. We were just talking."

"Well, she is probably ready for some food and a nap. Come on, let's get her down to the beach and I can feed her. She'll go to sleep and we can spend the afternoon alone soaking up the sun. You know, I will miss all the sunshine. I have grown quite fond of the clear and sunny days."

"I am sure you have, although it does not really matter to me, since I spent my days inside that hospital."

"I know, baby, and I am so sorry. Every time I came down here, it made me feel guilty because you were up there alone in that stale environment."

"Well, not anymore. I am leaving the past alone and it's time to focus on us and our family." They both smiled in agreement.

Julian and Aniyah spent the day at the beach enjoying the warm sunshine. It was an unforgettable experience. He had married the love of his life, and was now closing this chapter and opening the door to their brilliant future.

"Julian can you believe we are sitting on the beach in Hawaii with our baby, watching the sunset over the ocean?"

"No, I am still mystified. It's surreal."

"Are you ready to go? I want to eat at my favorite restaurant before we leave in the morning."

"I would not miss that for anything in the world. I'm ready. Oh… I just realized- no hospital food." Aniyah laughed. She was excited to have her husband alive and well.

Julian snatched up Olivia and headed for the car. A miracle cupped in the curve of his arm.

Chapter Fifteen:

Going Home

Aniyah and Julian packed their luggage, shipped the items they had collected over the last year and headed for the airport. It was one plane ride Julian found exhilarating. He kept busy on his laptop, working. Since his time in Hawaii, sales of their fitness clothing line had soared. Their waylaid plans could be activated once again. Julian's head was filled with marketing concepts to increase business. Plus, he looked forward to working with the local high school kids once again. It was a great opportunity to help them see the light, so to speak. After his near-death experience, he could teach from a whole new perspective. Not to mention, his ideas about real-estate investments could multiply their long-term passive income.

"Julian, can you take her for a while? My arm is falling asleep."

"Absolutely. I would be happy to take my baby girl." He packed up his laptop and snuggled with his daughter.

The silence felt comfortable, and before long Julian was day dreaming of the first 90 days in his dream job.

Not all opportunities are blessings. His big break turned out to be the worst experience of his life. Julian had a supervisor who demanded mandatory overtime, which was something that didn't exist. To make matters worse, his colleagues were inconsiderate and ignored his presence for the entire tour.

Since he was the new kid on the block, when Julian asked for assistance, he got the cold shoulder. The torment lasted two weeks before he went to a supervisor and asked to be assigned to another officer. Julian's request was granted; it was apparent the partnership was miserable.

It's important to have colleagues in close contact that have common similarities. Julian's new partner kept the work day fun. They were able to laugh and talk about job situations, go the gym before their shift and just relax. It seemed things were turning around, until a shift change came into play. Julian requested a later start time so he could get a chance to exercise before work. This pinged a sore spot with his new partner. Unbeknownst to Julian, he went straight to their supervisor and complained. Julian was called in to discuss the situation. The claim stated Julian was abandoning a coworker.

The conversation brought up a point Julian felt was unprofessional. He was informed that his job should always take precedence over his life, including his family. Everything happens for a reason. Julian was disgusted by the people in his department and their careless attitudes. Later in the week, he was called to the head supervisor's office and told a better position was available.

Julian's first day in the new position went better than expected. He kept working, but felt as though his supervisor had preconceived notions. During any conversation, Julian took a back seat. The men talked amongst themselves, leaving him feeling unwelcome.

One shift soon thereafter, Julian's partner came down with the flu and took a few days off work. Of course, he gave Julian the sickness, which forced him to take time off work. But while he was out sick, his supervisor turned in his time off slip. His partner failed to fill out a slip and it was swept under the rug, an unfair situation.

Julian felt his prior supervisor was spreading false rumors. The negativity caused other people in his department to look at him differently. Not to mention, he was the only African American on his team.

After a month in this unit, Julian was informed his work results were unacceptable, which was a lie. The outcome was the same for both parties; the reprimand was meant to force Julian to leave the unit. This point was proven when Julian's partner was issued a cell phone on the first day, yet Julian was left out. Needless to say, he was removed from the unit without valid reasoning.

When Julian asked for an explanation, he was told, "I don't have time to talk with you right now."

The situation proved that Julian had become a different person, and he was able to walk away without holding a grudge. He moved to a new unit and found himself openly accepted two days later; it was like a breath of fresh air.

Nevertheless, his time in the new unit was short-lived. A few days later, he was yet again assigned to another unit. Although it validated Julian's suspicions, the new position took him to an area that fell into his natural passions: helping the community. It was a chance to make a difference. The opportunity was bittersweet, but any situation in which he could serve to make someone's life better was a blessing. Julian survived the worst 90 days of his life, only to become the person his family adores today.

The flight attendants were gathering cups and food wrappers, which startled Julian out of his thoughts. He knew it was almost time for the plane to land. Aniyah looked exhausted; she had been through so much over the last year. Plus, being pregnant could not have been easy. Julian watched his two precious girls resting peacefully. He finally understood the plan God had for his life.

Aniyah had slept for the rest of their flight. "Honey, it's time to wake up. We have to get Olivia buckled in to land."

"Really, we are here already?" He nodded.

The pilot announced, "We are approaching O'Hare Airport. Please fasten your seatbelts and put your trays in the upright position." Their excitement overflowed.

Julian stepped off the plane into a familiar place. It was late afternoon, and the city was alive. Sofia had arranged to pick them up at the airport.

Since security was tight, only passengers were allowed in the terminals. Sofia was waiting in the baggage area for the family.

Aniyah heard her sister scream from a distance. She came running across the airport, ready to grab ahold of both of them. "I missed you so much!"

Aniyah hugged her sister tight. They had always been very close. "Julian... you look great!"

"Thank you, Sofia. It's good to be home."

"Let's grab the luggage and go home."

"Sounds like a perfect plan."

The sun was setting low on the horizon by the time they reached their home. It was a sight Julian wondered if he'd ever see again. Their neighbors had kept the house in pristine condition and they were excited to get home. But for some reason the traffic on their street was horrific; it was bumper to bumper with cars parked along the curb. Julian struggled to remember if this was normal. "Guys, where are all these cars from?"

"I know. It's crazy, right?" Sofia announced. Aniyah agreed but kept quiet.

The car pulled up to the house and Julian witnessed a sight he never imagined possible. Aniyah turned and smiled, "They are here for you, baby!"

Sofia stopped the car so Julian could get out. Over a hundred officers were standing at attention. They were lined up down the street all the way to his front door. It was the icing on the cake. Julian dropped to his knees, sobbing like a baby.

Aniyah put her hand on his shoulder. "Welcome home, baby!"

Julian looked up with tears in his eyes and took Aniyah's hand. He smiled and accepted the gracious homecoming celebration.

Olivia cooed for her daddy, and Julian stood up and grabbed the second love of his life. With the baby tucked in safe and Aniyah by his side, the life Julian sought was granted as promised. He realized you can't move forward and be successful while looking in the rearview mirror.

Additional Books from the Author
carmichaellewis.com

The Ultimate Teenagers Guide to Success: *What They Don't Teach You in School*

ISBN: 978-1952274008 Paperback
ISBN: 9781952274015 Epub

The Ultimate Teenager's Guide; Transformation through self-education will educate young people on how to set goals to achieve their dreams, how to manage and save their money and how to stay mentally and physically healthy. With this book, it will help create a vision for their life and help them define what success looks like to them.

As young as twelve years old, this book will inspire young people to discover their potential, teach them how to achieve financial independence, and how to succeed in school and beyond. This book will create a breed of healthy and wise adults who will protect the wellbeing of future generations. I sincerely believe that The Ultimate

Teenager's Guide will change the trajectory of many teenager's lives for the better.

It is our responsibility as a society to guard the wellbeing of our children. This book is one essential tool that will affect the lives of young people and the community as a whole.

Mira Mira – Look!

ISBN: 9781647864194 Hardcover
ISBN: 9781647869908 Paperback
ISBN: 9781648731402 Epub

Mira Mira-Look! shows how our household is teaching our son English and Spanish at the same time. By having a Hispanic mother and a black father, our son is learning how we are unique from traditional families.

Mira Mira- Look! teaches children a few common words they see daily. It introduces a second language and shows that children's curiosity sparks them to inquire about their environment... saying "Mira-Mira" in Spanish or "Look" in English. From our household to yours, we hope you enjoy Mira Mira- Look!

www.ingramcontent.com/pod-product-compliance
Lightning Source LLC
Chambersburg PA
CBHW052035070526
44584CB00016B/2046